Advance praise for *Living the Significant Life*

"Peter Hirsch and Robert Shemin have opened the door for thousands of people to enter into success. This book will inspire you to live every day with passion as you embrace your purpose."

—John C. Maxwell, author of *Developing the Leader within You*

"*Living the Significant Life* is an important book that will teach you how to get the most out of life—by giving. It is my privilege to count Peter Hirsch as a friend, and I can share with you that he lives these principles daily and with passion."

—Vicente Fox, president of Mexico, 2000–2006

"Peter's and Robert's teachings are stimulating and inspiring. They will encourage and excite you to the point of action. I especially love their insights on belief."

—Rudy Ruettiger, inspiration for the film *Rudy*

"This is a practical guide that demonstrates that genuine success—and significance—are measured as much by what we contribute to the world around us as by what we gain in money, titles and belongings."

—Sam Caster, founder of Mannatech and MannaRelief

"We yearn for success and significance. Unfortunately, we often pursue them in all the wrong ways. *Living the Significant Life* shows us how to achieve these things on God's terms and in a way that is not only personally rewarding but that also blesses others. The principles in this book are eternal, practical, and available to everyone who wants to reach for all that life has to offer."

—Bill McCartney, founder of Promise Keepers

"The world is round, and what you give will come back to you in measures beyond your imagination. I recommend these teachings and trainings to my organization and suggest you do the same."

—Bob Steed, CEO of Trivani International

"The simple truths this book teaches are a blueprint for living a life of purpose, success and significance."

—Jim Rohn, business philosopher and founder of Jim Rohn International

"Peter and Robert show us how to let go and let God change the meaning of our lives by design rather than delusion."

—Dr. Denis Waitley, author of *Seeds of Greatness*

"Living the Significant Life is a book that teaches what is really important—the intangibles that will inspire you to reach beyond your wildest dreams. I work very closely with Peter and know beyond a doubt that this book comes from his heart. He lives it, and so can you. I strongly recommend this book's teachings and trainings to our organization and suggest you do the same."

—Darren Jensen, Chief Sales Officer of Ampegy

"We have used Peter's trainings and ideas at Top Gun to focus and define our leadership to better serve all those we come in contact with. He will help you and your team strengthen your vision and leadership."

—Robert Dean Jr., Top Gun International

"It is not every day you read a book and immediately realize there is a different and better way to think about everyday life. This is one of those books. Take the time to read it and live it."

—Ken Hartwick, CEO of Just Energy

LIVING
the
SIGNIFICANT
LIFE

12 Principles for Making a Difference

PETER HIRSCH
ROBERT SHEMIN

WILEY

John Wiley & Sons, Inc.

Published by John Wiley & Sons, Inc., Hoboken, New Jersey
Published simultaneously in Canada

Limit of Liability/Disclaimer of Warranty: While the publisher and the author have used their best efforts in preparing this book, they make no representations or warranties with respect to the accuracy or completeness of the contents of this book and specifically disclaim any implied warranties of merchantability or fitness for a particular purpose. No warranty may be created or extended by sales representatives or written sales materials. The advice and strategies contained herein may not be suitable for your situation. You should consult with a professional where appropriate. Neither the publisher nor the author shall be liable for any loss of profit or any other commercial damages, including but not limited to special, incidental, consequential, or other damages.

For general information about our other products and services, please contact our Customer Care Department within the United States at (800) 762–2974, outside the United States at (317) 572–3993 or fax (317) 572–4002.

Wiley also publishes its books in a variety of electronic formats and by print-on-demand. Some content that appears in standard print versions of this book may not be available in other formats. For more information about Wiley products, visit us at www.wiley.com.

Hirsch, Peter, date.
   Living the significant life: 12 principles for making a difference/Peter Hirsch and Robert Shemin.
      p. cm.
   Includes bibliographical references and index.
   ISBN 978-0-470-64125-5 (pbk); ISBN 978-1-118-17513-2 (ebk);
ISBN 978-1-118-17514-9 (ebk); ISBN 978-1-118-17515-6 (ebk)
   1. Meaning (Psychology).   2. Self-actualization (Psychology).   I. Shemin, Robert, date.   II. Title.
   BF463.M4H57 2012
   158—dc23

                                                        2011049810

Printed in the United States of America

10 9 8 7 6 5 4 3 2 1

For Ariel & Malia
—P. H.

For Alexander
—R. S.

Contents

Foreword

Living the Significant Life is a book that shares some principles all of us should adopt and why we should adopt them. This is a book that gives clear insights, thoughts, and directions that will make a difference in anyone's life.

It's common sense, written from the heart, based on personal experience and a study of significance. The authors, as the saying goes, have "been there and done that." Now they want you to come along with them. Not only do they want you to do that, they also give compelling reasons why the approach they're taking will enrich and enhance every phase of your life, making you a happier, healthier, and better person as you battle the difficulties that very frequently come with life.

The powerful principles that *Living the Significant Life* examines have worked for thousands of people, and I have every reason to believe they can work for you as well. As a matter of fact, when I adopted many of these principles that the authors discuss with such passion, every facet of my life was affected and enriched.

I encourage you to pick up your pen when you pick up this book. Mark the passages that have meaning for you. Pause, reflect on, and *really* think about them. Then write yourself a little note, a reminder of something you can use that will make you a better person and a more complete human being—one able to harness the power instilled inside you.

I encourage you not to pick up this book with the intention of "finishing" it; instead, read the book with the purpose of gleaning wisdom from it that will enrich your life increasingly with every subsequent reading. The enrichment begins when you follow the directions and suggestions. So take the steps the authors are encouraging, and I really will see you—not just *at* the top but *over* the top!

—Zig Ziglar

Acknowledgments

We'd like to thank our families for their continuous love, encouragement, and support while we traveled the world sharpening these principles. In addition, our literary agent, David Hale Smith, has been a source of constant wisdom, and so have the staff and editors at John Wiley & Sons. We are grateful to Susan McDonald, who turns our thoughts and stories into coherent sentences and chapters. Finally, we thank our friends around the country and around the globe, who challenge us to live each day with passion and purpose.

From Success to Significance

Success is what happens *to* you; significance
is what happens *through* you.
—*Peter Hirsch*

Dane Wierman didn't get a lot of birthday presents for his eighth birthday, but don't feel sorry for him— that's the way he wanted it! Instead of buying presents for him, his friends were asked to donate the money they would have spent on gifts to the children of Guatemala.

Let's back up a bit. Shortly before Dane's birthday, his father, Dr. Troy Wierman, had returned from a medical mission to Guatemala with stories about the dire needs of the people he had met there. Dane was touched and wanted to find some way to share what he had with the Guatemalan children who had so little. When he heard that a friend had used his birthday party to raise money for a classmate's surgery, Dane decided that this was what he wanted to do for the children of Guatemala. And that's exactly what he did.

Dane raised $360 and gave it all to a medical clinic's milk program. Instead of a gaming system or a motorized scooter, Dane bought milk and meals for starving children.

That's significance.

Now let us tell you a little about the medical team that inspired Dane's generosity.

After a long and bumpy trip, the team arrived at a remote village in the Quiche district. The team's doctors and nurses briefly laid down their stethoscopes and picked up brooms and cleaning supplies to prepare the dirt-filled cement area that would become the well-equipped mobile medical clinic. Within an hour, the exam areas were clean, patients were checked in, the pharmacy was well stocked, and a small school bus was converted into a sonogram facility and a functioning laboratory.

At the same time the medical team was seeing hundreds of patients, a construction team of twenty men and women set out to build a new dorm at a nearby orphanage. The crew was made up of people of all ages and included office workers, salespeople, firefighters, and a few who actually knew construction. What the team didn't know was that just days before their arrival, one of the orphanage buildings had caught fire and had been completely destroyed. There were, thank goodness, no children in the building at the time. The children and the local community watched in amazement as the team of construction "pros" poured their hearts into completing a new dorm in just two days. The team also left a large supply of lumber, bedding, clothes, school supplies, and canned food—enough to supply the orphanage until the team fulfilled its commitment to return in just a few months.

That's significance.

Meanwhile, thirteen hundred miles away in Texas, a group of people were putting on a one-day garage sale. They put up a giant banner on a prominent corner in Plano. Let's be very clear: if you have a garage sale anywhere in North Dallas, suddenly traffic comes from every direction. People want to see what you no longer want.

But this was unlike any other garage sale anybody had ever seen before, because it wasn't actually a sale. Everything—every item—was completely free. The signs had advertised that each person could take five things—totally free. People came. Boy, did people come.

Exciting things began to happen. Let us share just two of them.

A blind single mother and her seven-year-old daughter came to the sale. The little girl, Becca, didn't have a winter coat, and her mother had been praying that she would find one for her. When they arrived, they discovered that three brand-new coats had been donated. Becca tried on the one she liked best, and it fit perfectly. Her mother started crying for joy when she heard the delight in her daughter's voice as she talked about how beautiful it was.

Becca was so excited that she asked one of the workers if she could get something for her mother, too, so the worker took her aside, and Becca secretly picked out a gift to give her mother for Christmas. Meanwhile, the mother had turned to one of the workers and said, "I want to get a Christmas gift for my daughter." Neither knew what the other was doing.

That's significance.

Elsewhere at the garage "sale," after picking out several items, two women mentioned that they would like to have one of the large brass beds that was on display, but they didn't have a way to get it home. One of the workers immediately spoke up and said, "We'll deliver it to your home right now—totally free." The women looked stunned and one said, "What kind of people are you?" They were shocked by the power of love in action.

That, too, is significance.

It may not fit a classic definition of personal success. It may not be on the front pages of newspapers. But it's something that touches people's lives. It's something happening through you to touch someone else.

Whether it takes place in Guatemala or Texas or anywhere else in the world, the global definition of success is changing. We are a people in need of significance.

As this is being written, our country is struggling to emerge from a global economic tsunami. The Dow Jones Industrial Average is plunging one day and shooting up some the next, home foreclosures are at a record level, fear is at an all-time high for the average investor, and our children's future has been mortgaged with unimaginable federal debt. Who can you trust with your hard-earned money?

With the evening news offering little to smile about, it's no wonder that all this upheaval is having an effect on our mental and emotional health. We worry about our ability to retire comfortably, to provide a life for our children that matches the one our parents provided for us, to make a positive difference in the world, and to find the personal joy that each of us deserves.

So all of this leads to some questions: What is it that we truly desire? How do we define success in this chaotic universe? We think the answer is that we need to *redefine* success.

We are a people hungry for change. We are a people thirsty for more. We are a people in need of significance. It's true: it's significance that people are searching for, not success—at least not the traditional definition of success.

Now don't get us wrong: there's nothing inherently wrong with success and wanting to be successful. In fact, this entire book explores principles that have the power to make you more successful, happier, and more fulfilled. However, it is our firm belief that significance—what happens through you, not to you—is what success is all about. How do you make *others* successful, and, in turn, yourself?

TIPS FROM PETER

I was a success. By almost any definition, I had made it. I graduated at the top of my class in law school when I was twenty-four. That year, I went to work for one of the country's most prestigious law firms and was earning a six-figure salary.

No doubt about it. I was a "success." But I wasn't happy.

The self-serving life of a New York City litigation attorney left me feeling empty, depressed, and alone. For the first time in my life, I felt utterly powerless. For weeks, I couldn't sleep. I didn't understand why this was happening to me. Everyone around me was telling me how successful and promising my career was, but I couldn't see it. The "success" meant nothing to me, and I didn't know why.

To this day, I can't tell you exactly what happened, but I made a choice that forever changed my life. I discovered that true success comes only to those who are invested in the success of others. That's significance. Success is what happens to you; significance is what happens through you.

My first book, *Living with Passion*, was a success. Some may even call it significant. Still, its focus was on success—what the reader could get from it.

The stories that open this book are amazing because they involve ordinary people who decided to make a difference. What would the world look like if everyone felt that way? The reality is that most people do. Most of us yearn to make a difference, have an impact, leave a legacy. Here's the challenge. It's called life. Yes, all of us would like to do "good," but by the time we get home from work, feed the kids, walk the dog, and do the dishes, we simply forget about the good we wanted to do all day. What if doing good is what you did for a living?

For the last five years, my passion has been teaching individuals and companies about Social Entrepreneurship. Simply defined, Social Entrepreneurship uses entrepreneurship and for-profit principles to solve global, social issues. It empowers ordinary people to make an extraordinary impact.

The challenge we face today is that the old giving model is largely broken. As the economy impacts people's lives around the world, giving to churches, ministries, and other nonprofit organizations has decreased dramatically. Some of the most important organizations in the world are nearing extinction. The times call for a new solution. The needs are getting greater, yet the resources appear to be diminishing. How can the two be reconciled? It's going to take different and creative thinking. The world's great challenges are getting worse, so what can we do?

It's time for the for-profit world to come up with the solutions. Hundreds of companies are now stepping up to battle social issues. Toms Shoes has revolutionized giving through their buy-one-give-one program. Grameen Bank is having a powerful impact on poverty through microloans. Mannatech and Nu-Skin International are nourishing thousands upon thousands of children. Energy companies such as Ampegy and Spark Energy are giving power to the powerless. All of these for-profit companies are inviting consumers to be part of the solution. They are offering a solution that we can call, for lack of a better term, "Compassionate Consumption."

Social Entrepreneurship has four elements (the first two are shared by all entrepreneurs):

- See the problem.
- Find or create the solution.
- Tap into people's passion.
- Incentivize them to be part of the solution.

The reality is that something has to change. The old fund-raising efforts of asking people to spend money they don't have on stuff they don't need just isn't working anymore. It's time to invite people to seriously be part of the solution.

This book is different from my first because I'm different. My focus has changed. My passion has changed. My passion today is helping others to learn the benefits of living a significant life.

A Word about Our Method

You're about to begin exploring the twelve principles that will help you to move from wherever you are now into a life of significance and fulfillment, but first we'd like to introduce you to some friends of ours.

Are you familiar with the song "Every Picture Tells a Story"? We happen to believe that the opposite is also true: every story paints a picture. That's why we've created a series of stories— parables, actually—to illustrate the twelve principles. At the end of each chapter, we'll see how some fictional characters deal with the kinds of issues all of us face from time to time, and we'll watch them use the principles outlined in this book to successfully navigate the sometimes murky waters of their lives.

Our hope is that by letting us share their experiences, the characters who inhabit these stories will paint a picture to show how you can apply these principles to your own life.

Intensify Your Desire

Ignore what a man desires and you ignore
the very source of his power.
—*Walter Lippmann*

Have you ever reached a point in your life or work when you realized you were not where you wanted to be? Have you ever stopped and noticed that you could be doing more, achieving more, and experiencing more success, happiness, and fulfillment?

Have you ever wondered what it would be like to go beyond making incremental gains in your performance or in the quality of your life and work—to rocket past your previous limitations and make a real breakthrough? That's the possibility of living a significant life. And it's all yours; all you have to do is develop the desire and play with it.

The fine art of desire and perseverance is beautifully expressed in the popular song by reggae artist Jimmy Cliff, "You Can Get It If You Really Want."

What's great about these lyrics is the clarity. We don't think the song would have been anywhere near as successful if Jimmy had instead written, "You can get it if you sort of want," or "You can get it if you halfway want," or "You can get it if you, well, don't really want, but somebody else said it was a fine idea, and besides, it's an appropriate thing to want for someone with your income and standing in the community, and what's more, your mother would approve as well, and . . ."

You get the idea. The only way you get anything is if you *really want*. Don't want, halfway want, sort of want, and all those other less than, quasi-wants just won't cut it. If you're going to "succeed at last," you've got to *want* to.

Wanting to Want

Real wanting unfortunately has a number of impostors to contend with. The cleverest of these false wants is *wanting* to want.

We know so many people who suffer from this. It's so debilitating and limiting, because it looks for all the world as though it's the same as really wanting something—but it's not.

Some people spend their whole lives *wanting to want* to live somewhere else, work at some other career that they'd dearly love, do this, or have that, but it's all an illusion. It's just busywork masquerading as productivity.

Wanting to want is avoiding, holding back, and fearing the unknown. It's stating goals that sound good, but not really being committed to them. It's confusing aspirations with wishful thinking. It's probably fear of failure as much as anything—a form of procrastination that allows the person to look good in the process of doing nothing productive, except going through the motions.

Real wanting is something very different. It's a powerful, inspiring urge, and as such, there is something divinely inspired about it.

Neither of us puts much stock in spiritual and personal growth practices that maintain that the only way to an "enlightened" life is through ridding oneself of all desire. On the contrary, desire, genuine wanting, is a gift from God, a powerful and compelling tool for accomplishment. Desire is a human birthright and very much directly linked to (indeed, responsible for) all the extraordinary and exciting progress that humans have made throughout the millennia of our existence on this planet. Of course, we've taken some wrong turns and made some errors of both judgment and action. But it is our *desire*—especially when it appears collectively—to right those wrongs that inspires the process to a new and better result.

The Creative Force of Desire

Like any other quality we'll talk about in this book, desire has no color of its own. That's up to each of us individually. Desire for more than is appropriate, or for greater than you deserve, is greed. And desire for less than you deserve is often an expression of a self-defeating, no-possibility *habitude* (habit combined with attitude), born of low self-worth and low self-esteem.

Clearly, genuine desire is powerful. Developing the ability to harness its strength for good and not for harm is the challenge. Robert Fritz, in *The Path of Least Resistance*, gives practical insights into the accomplishment process. His explanation of how we get what we desire is particularly impressive.

When we have a desire for something, but what we have at present is different from the fulfillment of that desire, there is a natural tension that develops. This condition is subject to the natural law that tension seeks resolution.

Picture a stretched rubber band. The tension in that rubber band acts almost as though it *wants* to relax, to resolve the tension and go back to its resting state. So it is when we desire something we do not have. There is a tension, stretched between our current condition and the desired condition, that seeks to be resolved. The bigger the desire, the greater the tension.

The helpful part is that this tension is not only a natural occurrence, it is also the force we use to get what we want—whether or not we are aware of its presence. As long as we continue to encourage and maintain that tension, it's there for us, naturally and powerfully bringing our desire into being. Fritz shows that even though people often experience such tension as something stressful, it can be used and experienced as the powerful inspirational force it really is.

Now let's do something really fascinating with Fritz's rubber band imagery.

Think of what you have in your life now as the end of the rubber band that's in your left hand, and think of your desire as the end that's in your right hand. Now stretch the rubber band out to represent the difference (that is, the distance) between the two.

With your present condition and your desired future being pulled away from each other as you stretch the rubber band, what's going to happen next? How will you influence in which direction the tension resolves?

Let go of the right side (your desire). The tension relaxes the rubber band over to your left hand. This is like letting go of your desire. That's one way to resolve the tension: give up your dreams, forget about what you want. When you do, what you end up with is just what you already had: your present condition.

In this case, letting the rubber band's tension relax means resignation: nothing's changed, your dreams are futile, you give up and stick with the status quo. Many people accept that condition in order to escape the tension that is naturally produced by having dreams and aspirations unfulfilled.

But what if you do it the other way around? What happens if you let go of the left-hand end of the rubber band? Now what remains is your desire.

What you have now, what Fritz calls "current reality," will do one thing you can always count on: it will change; everything always does. So if you hold onto your desire, if you make it strong through the principles we'll be talking about later—belief in yourself, an upbeat habitude, focus, letting go of your fears—you can direct and even accelerate the changes in your current circumstances, moving from what you have now to what you genuinely desire!

Think about it for just a moment. What you have now will change—that's a given. It's changing right now even as you read this. If you hold onto and make powerful the desire for what you want, the tension will most likely resolve naturally in favor of your desires.

There are two keys to this: telling the truth about what you have now, and telling the truth about what you desire. Affirmations and positive thinking can be powerful tools, but lying to yourself is dangerous. So be honest with yourself about what it is you really want. Then keep the tension alive so that its natural power is working for you to accomplish your desire.

Isn't that fantastic?

Once you have the intense desire to achieve whatever it is you want to achieve, and inspiration itself is your ally, you are unstoppable. If your desire is truly intense—what we call *burning desire*—and you are single-mindedly aiming toward your goals, no one and nothing can sidetrack you. The key is to know exactly what you are seeking and what you really, really want.

Building Rapport

Once you've cultivated an intense and burning desire, you can communicate this desire to others, and when you do that, you supercharge the entire accomplishment process. The more people you enroll in your desire, the more inspirational power you have to accomplish your dreams.

You transfer your beliefs to others through the following three ways:

1. Your words
2. Your voice inflection
3. Your body language

These three forms of communication combine to form the skill we call *building rapport*.

When you learn the skill of establishing rapport with unlimited numbers of people, you will develop an infinite variety of avenues for the experience and expression of joy, happiness, and success in your life and your work—and perhaps most important, in theirs. In essence, building rapport simply means establishing the most commonality and comfort possible in a relationship.

Most human beings have a fascinating behavioral quality: we like people who like us. Abraham Lincoln said, "If you would win a man to your cause, first convince him that you are his friend."

We spend time with and feel comfortable with those people who share our interests and passions. Even people who have difficulty talking to strangers will do so easily if there is an obvious commonality between them, such as the fact that they are both riding mountain bikes or that they're both wearing jazz dance shoes or baseball caps from the same team.

Most people establish rapport with words, by asking questions to reveal areas of common interest or personal similarities. But this is a far more limited basis for rapport-building than it might seem because of the often overlooked fact that words mean different things to different people. We all have our own definitions for words and unique interpretations for the same set of facts. If five people view the same event, you'll have five different descriptions of what happened.

However, when you use rapport-building skills, you can guarantee making a connection with others. Can you see any value for you in being able to establish rapport instantly in a variety of personal and professional encounters? It really is powerful. Let's take a brief look at some rapport-building skills you can use easily and immediately.

Mirroring and Matching

It's important to realize how little our communication is composed of words. In fact, some widely respected research conducted years ago by the Pacific Institute in Seattle found that our communication is actually 93 percent nonverbal. That is, words themselves compose only 7 percent—about one-fourteenth!—of our total communication.

If words represent such a small part of our communication, where does the other thirteen-fourteenths come from? More than in any other way, people judge you and make decisions about how they think and feel about you based on your voice inflection and body language.

When you mirror and match the inflection and body language of the person you're talking with, you develop instant rapport— no matter what is being said. People are most open and comfortable with other people who are like them. Mirroring and matching is a practice in which you observe and adopt some of the dominant characteristics of the person with whom you're speaking.

You might think that this technique is too obvious or seems phony, that you will come off as strange or even be perceived as mocking the other person, but that's not the case. What we're doing here is actually quite subtle, and it communicates almost entirely on a subconscious level.

The truth is that we mirror and match each other all the time. When people around us start to yawn or laugh, we often start to yawn or laugh. It's something you already do naturally and automatically, at least to some extent. Our purpose here is simply to have you recognize that fact and focus on it—to bring it out of the realm of the subconscious so you can begin to use mirroring and matching with awareness and discipline to achieve the results you're after.

Let's start with your voice.

Your Voice

Your voice inflection composes 38 percent of your communication with others. There are four aspects of your voice that can be looked at separately: tone, tempo, volume, and vocabulary.

Tone is a quality apart from how fast or slow and how quietly or loudly you talk. Here are some examples of different tones: excited, dry, laid-back, thoughtful, hurried, enthusiastic. What you call the tone of a person's voice is subjective and unimportant. What matters is to observe the tone being used and to emulate the same tone in your conversation with that person.

Tempo is the speed at which a person is talking. Your goal is simply to match the pace and pattern of the other person's speech.

Volume, like tempo, is self-explanatory. Speak softly with soft-spoken men and women, louder with those whose volume is greater.

Vocabulary is your choice of words. Notice the key words the other person uses and use them in your conversation as well. Especially important are words or phrases that give you the person's predominant thinking orientation, such as when he or she says, "I think," "I feel," "I see," or "I hear what you're saying." Although you may be a thinker, when you're with someone whose orientation is that of a feeler, match that in your conversation by shifting what you normally say from "I think" to "I feel."

TIPS FROM PETER

I normally speak quite quickly and fairly loudly. I also tend to say "I think" a lot, and I often use a number of other key words you might recognize from reading this book: *passion, focus, choice, purpose, encourage, inspire, power, service, success,* and *significance,* among others.

Now, if you came up to me speaking fast, excited, and in a strong presentation voice and said, "Peter, this is great! I think we can really inspire lots of people to greater happiness and fulfillment, to surpass their limitations and fears by focusing on having a choice in all that they do and say, by connecting them with what they're truly passionate about in their lives," I would conclude that you are a very intelligent, high-integrity person who's really up to great things in your life. I would like you and respect you immediately, and I would want to spend time with you, talking and sharing more ideas together.

Back in law school, long before I learned about any of these communication skills, I had an amazing experience that I wondered about for years afterward—until I discovered the mirroring and matching technology.

I was a top student, used to getting all As. We had a midterm exam in tort law, and as I emerged from the classroom I knew I had aced the exam. I even had the thought that I had been so brilliant, they were surely going to invite me to be on the faculty.

I got a C–! I couldn't believe it! Me, Peter "L-is-for-Lawyer" Hirsch, with a C– on my law exam. I was stunned!

I went immediately to the law library and checked out every book and paper my tort professor had ever written. I studied these books and papers for the remaining weeks of the semester. When it came time for the finals, I knew every word, phrase, and manner of expression my professor had used—and I put them all into the exam paper.

How did I do? You can guess. This time I got an A.

I'm convinced that there was no difference between the substance of my midterm and that of my final. All that changed was the fact that my expression on the final matched that of my professor. Therefore, he was more comfortable with me and probably thought to himself, "Ah, now there's a student who really understands the material!"

Mirroring and matching is the most powerful way in the world to have people on your side, open and wanting to share with you who they are and what they're up to.

Your Body Language

Body language represents 55 percent of your communication. There are so many aspects of body language you can mirror: people's gestures, posture, relationship to the surrounding space, breathing, touch, movement, facial expression, and much more.

As you begin to mirror and match another person's body language—hand movements in gestures, facial expressions, posture, distance of standing and sitting in relation to you— you'll discover an amazing thing. You will actually begin to feel the way the other person is feeling.

Stop, Look, and Listen

The importance of mirroring and matching is that it tells us something interesting about our habitual communication styles: most of us talk too much!

It's true. People generally talk much more than they listen, but we actually learn only when we're listening; we learn nothing by talking. We've heard it many times before: the Talmudic teaching that we've been given two ears and one mouth because we're supposed to listen twice as much as we talk has a lot of merit.

If you're going to succeed in any relationship or business enterprise, you've got to care about people. Perhaps you've heard the expression "People won't care about how much you know till they know how much you care." It is quite true, and the best—and quickest—way in the world to show people how much you care is by listening.

There is nothing more effective for raising people's self-esteem, self-confidence, and self-worth than showing them we care, and we do this primarily by listening—*really* listening.

That isn't as easy as it might sound. Focusing on another person means shutting down everything on your own list, paying complete attention and hearing every word the other person says. Some people call this "listening without an agenda." It means setting aside your own concerns, your evaluation in process of that person and what he or she is saying, and simply listening.

There's a great expression that speaks directly to this point: "The mind is like a parachute: it's of no use unless it's open."

Listening to people openly—not thinking about what you are going to say next—without the inside-the-mind comments is the most effective way to show people you care, and it's the very best way in the world to learn and encourage.

Make a commitment to be aware of the importance of listening to people. Be aware of body language—yours and theirs. When appropriate, lean forward, smile, and put interest and attention in your eyes. This lets people know that you are fully present with them and are invested in their self-worth (as well as your own); it affirms their importance to you and gives them confidence in you.

It is vitally important to let people feel safe in opening up to you—and the best way to do that is by asking questions.

The Right Questions

There are two types of questions: open-ended and closed. Open-ended questions can lead to all sorts of places and open up possibilities. Closed questions lead nowhere. They ask for nothing more than one specific answer—usually yes or no. They are like emotional short circuits.

We gain very little information from closed questions: "Well, Bob, did you like the training?"

Whether Bob answers, "Yes, I did," or "No, not really," the conversation still goes *clunk!* You really haven't moved forward at all. This is because closed questions are not structured to reveal people's genuine desires. Open-ended questions do just that: "Bob, what was the best part of the training for you?"

It is only when you understand other people's desires that you will be able to see how you can benefit them. Always remember that's what people care about: how you can benefit them, what your value is to them.

The worst mistake that anyone who deals with people can make is to talk facts, figures, and statistics. Nobody really cares about them. People want benefits, and benefits alone. People are after value—we are all value-driven homing devices.

Last year hundreds of thousands of refrigerators were sold in the United States. And guess what? Not one person actually *wanted* a refrigerator!

What they really wanted was fresh food, cold food, and frozen food. They wanted the convenience of food stocked up near them so they could fix meals without having to go out to shop every day. They wanted the *benefits* that a refrigerator would bring them: fresh vegetables, food that lasts longer, cool drinks, ice cream, and so forth.

Do you know how many drill bits are sold every year in this country? Millions. Do you know what every one of those drill-bit buyers is really after? They don't want drill bits. They want holes.

When you ask questions, ask those that give you the greatest opportunity to really listen; questions that cause people to tell you what they want, what their feelings are; questions that reveal their desires and how you can help them achieve them.

Asking open-ended questions also provides you with a fringe benefit: you will find yourself living everyday life with much more interest and involvement. People are like snowflakes: there are no two exactly alike. If you give people time and attention, if you listen to them, and if you reveal their desires, they will open up to you. They will come into partnership with you in a combined effort to achieve all of your goals and theirs as well. That kind of powerful, inspiring relationship with others is a major key to success and happiness.

"Mom! Mom! *Mom!*"

Justin burst into the house like a freight train. He'd run all the way from the bus stop at breakneck speed and now tore through the house, looking for his mother.

"I'm in the kitchen," his mother, Christine, called, but Justin was already flying into the room.

"Igettogotospacecamp! Igettogotospacecamp!" he said.

"What? Slow down."

"I get to go to space camp! The one where you get to spend a whole week learning about space and astronauts and planets, and I get to go!"

Justin had been fascinated by space for years. It had started simply enough when he'd received a book about the planets for his fifth birthday. He'd looked through the photos and illustrations over and over, and the book had become mandatory reading each night before he went to bed. Although he wasn't able to read most of the words, it hadn't been long before he'd memorized the entire text. More books followed, plus toy rockets, astronaut Halloween costumes, and a collection of posters that covered the walls of his bedroom. Now, at age nine, he knew more about the solar system than most adults, and he followed every space shuttle mission like a religion.

"Okay, hold on a minute," Christine said. "Slow down and explain this to me."

Justin took a deep breath. "Okay. You know my science teacher, Mrs. Kirwin?" He paused, waiting for confirmation that his mother did indeed know his teacher.

"Yes, I know Mrs. Kirwin," Christine said with a smile.

"Okay. Well, she's organizing a trip to space camp this summer. You have to be at least nine to go, and now that we're nine, we're old enough."

"This trip is for your whole class?"

"Yeah, anybody who wants to go. Well, I guess not anybody. She can only take fifteen kids, so the first fifteen who sign up get to go." He reached into his backpack and pulled out a manila envelope. "Here, you have to read this stuff, and you and Dad have to fill out some papers. I can go, right? Please?"

"Well, your dad and I have to read this information and see how much it costs, but it sounds like a good opportunity."

"Okay, you'll talk about it as soon as he gets home?"

"We'll look at the papers after dinner, I promise."

"Great. I'm going to call Nick and tell him I can probably go."

"Okay, but homework starts in fifteen minutes," Christine said, but Justin had already disappeared from the kitchen.

During dinner, Justin chattered animatedly about his upcoming adventure. He'd looked up information about the camp online and learned about the activities for his age group. "We get to learn all about Mars and pretend that we really go on a trip there," he said. "We get to do experiments and collect rocks and other stuff. And we get to meet a real astronaut. I'm going to tell him that I'm going to be an astronaut, too."

Later that evening, Justin's father, Steve, found his wife sitting at the kitchen table with the papers about the trip spread out in front of her. "How does it sound?" he asked.

"It sounds great," Christine replied. "Two teachers will be going, so it's well supervised, and the program sounds like something Justin would really love."

"And the big question: How much does it cost?"

"The fee is eight hundred dollars, but listen to this. The kids have to earn the money before they can go. Parents aren't allowed to foot the bill directly."

"Well, that's a first," Steve said with a laugh. "How is a nine-year-old supposed to earn eight hundred dollars?"

"The school is organizing several fundraising opportunities for them. Selling wrapping paper, selling poinsettias for Christmas, selling those discount coupon books for restaurants, several things like that."

"That's a lot of selling, especially for a shy kid like Justin."

"What's a lot of selling?" asked Justin as he came into the room.

"We're talking about your trip," Christine said. "You and the other kids have to earn the money before you can go. Parents aren't allowed to just pay for it. I guess they think it will make you appreciate it more."

"What do I have to do?" Justin asked. His demeanor changed rapidly as his mother explained the fundraisers. "Who would I sell all that stuff to?"

"You could go door-to-door in the neighborhood, maybe call the parents of your friends who don't want to go on the trip, ask people at church."

"Can't you guys just give the money and say I earned it?"

"Sorry, kiddo," Steve said. "You have to turn in the information about who bought your stuff, and besides, that wouldn't be honest, would it?"

"I guess not," Justin said.

Several days later, Christine was putting Justin's lunch into his backpack when she saw a thick envelope inside. Pulling it out, she discovered that it was the sales packet for the wrapping-paper drive.

"Justin, how long have you had this?" she asked.

"A couple of days, I guess."

"We need to get started on this right away."

Justin didn't say anything.

"What's wrong? You still want to go to space camp, right?" Christine asked.

"Sure, but I don't want to sell all that junk. It's going to be hard, and I don't like talking to adults."

"I'm an adult. You don't have any trouble talking to me."

"You're my mom. That doesn't count. I have to go before I miss the bus."

"Okay, we'll talk more about this tonight. Have a good day."

That evening, Steve and Christine sat down with Justin and his sales packet. As they made a list of the people he could approach, Justin looked like he was being tortured.

Christine put her hand on her son's shoulder and spoke quietly. "Look, honey, I know how hard it is for you to do things like this, but sometimes we have to do things that are hard for us. It's just part of life. You're getting older, and you need to start learning that if you want something badly enough, you have to work for it, even if it means doing something that makes you uncomfortable."

"Your mom's right," Steve said. "You've wanted to go to space camp since the day you found out it existed. Now you've got a chance to go. I guess the question is, how badly do you want it?"

"Real bad," Justin admitted. "More than anything."

"Then I guess you're going to have to prove that by working for it," Steve said.

"What would I say to people? I don't know how to sell stuff," Justin said.

"We'll help you figure out what to say. And maybe we should start with somebody easy, like your grandfather. You don't have any trouble talking to him, and it would be good practice," Steve said.

"Do you think Grandpa needs wrapping paper? He usually just gives us money on our birthdays."

"I think he wants his grandson to go to space camp," Steve said with a smile.

Ten minutes later, Justin had made his first sale. "I'll take five rolls," Christine's father had said. "You pick out some paper you think I'd like, and I'll stop by with a check tomorrow." That had been easy.

Justin's confidence didn't last long. His grandfather was easy to talk to. Other people would be hard.

"How badly do you want to go, Justin?" Steve asked again. "Five rolls of wrapping paper won't get you to space camp. Tomorrow you're going to have to go around to the neighbors and start asking them."

Christine's heart broke for her son. She knew what it was like to be shy, but she also knew how much space camp meant to him. This was a perfect opportunity for him, and he'd be sorry later if he let it pass. Maybe there was a way to ease him along gradually.

"I've got an idea," she said. "How about if we start with something easier than going door-to-door? Your school directory has e-mail addresses for most of the parents. What if we sent an e-mail to some of the parents of kids in the other grades? Your dad and I could help you write it. You'd explain what you're selling, tell them about the trip to space camp and how much you want to go, and ask if they're interested in seeing your wrapping paper catalog. If they are, you can arrange a time to go over and show it to them. That way, when you got to their houses, they'd already know why you were there, and you wouldn't have to explain it to them. Would that make it easier?"

"Yeah, I guess I could do that," Justin said.

By bedtime, Justin had e-mailed his sales pitch to about two dozen parents. He went to sleep looking at his posters and thinking that he might get to space camp after all.

Arriving home from school the next day, Justin eagerly went to the computer and found several responses to his e-mail. A few politely said they didn't need any wrapping paper, but five people said they were interested and invited him to come over with his catalog. His excitement turned to dread when he realized what he had to do next: phone five strangers, then go to their houses and talk to them in person.

"Don't worry," Christine said. "I've got this handled."

She sat down with Justin and helped him write a short script: "Hello, this is Justin Finch. Thank you for answering my e-mail about the wrapping paper. I really want to go to space camp, and this will help me a lot. Could I come over tomorrow after school and show you the catalog?" After practicing his spiel a few times, he made the first call, then the other four. He had five appointments.

The following afternoon, Christine was waiting when Justin got home from school. They spent a few minutes practicing the conversations he might have with his customers, then headed out to the car, where Justin found a bag on his seat.

"It's for you," Christine said. "Open it."

Justin opened the bag and pulled out two books. The first one, *A Complete History of the American Space Program*, was beyond his reading level, but he didn't care. It was filled with photos tracing every development in the country's space exploration efforts, and a pocket in the back held a DVD with eight hours of footage. The second book was *Careers in Space*. This one was much closer to his reading level, and it described a wide range of career choices in the aeronautics and space industries. Justin planned to become an astronaut, but some of those engineering jobs looked pretty cool, too.

"Thanks, Mom!" he said.

"You're welcome," Christine replied. "Here's what I'm thinking. The only way you're going to get to space camp next summer is by selling enough wrapping paper and other things to earn the money, and the only way you're going to do that is by wanting it badly enough. I know how hard this is for you, but I also know how much you want this trip, so I thought these books might be a good reminder for you. You can look through them while we're driving to your customers' houses and think about how much fun you'll have at space camp, especially since you'll be going with your friends and Mrs. Kirwin. Every time you have to call someone and ask them to buy something, or go to the neighbors' houses, or approach people at church, you can use the books to remind you about what you're working for and how much you want it. Do you think that might help?"

"Yeah, maybe so. You're pretty smart, Mom."

"Remember that when you're a teenager," Christine said with a laugh.

When Justin returned to the car after visiting his first customer, Christine asked, "How did it go?"

"Good. She was real nice and she bought four rolls," he said as he clicked his seat belt into place and picked up one of his books. "I told her I'd be back when we get the order forms for those poinsettia things."

We've all been in Justin's situation at one time or another, haven't we? We've wanted something so much we could almost taste it, yet we had to slay a few dragons to attain it. As any knight worth his armor will tell you, it's a lot easier to slay dragons when what's waiting on the other side of the forest is something you desire with all your heart, something that speaks to your true purpose. Justin's story focuses on some of the major themes of this chapter—really wanting something, and genuine listening. Don't disregard the other main theme of building rapport. Throughout this book, we illustrate certain themes and not others simply because of time and text constraints.

Let's talk about that next.

Find Your Purpose

Great minds have purposes; others have wishes.
—*Washington Irving*

I *need* a reason!" The reason we are doing something—anything—is of utmost importance. If the reasons are clear, the rest will make itself known. People who know *why* they are doing something inevitably outperform people who know *how*; people who know how usually work for people who know why. As King Solomon wrote, "Without a vision, we perish."

The people we are and everything we do are inspired by our purpose and values.

Take a look at any trouble in the world: rival factions in a warring country, rivalry between corporate competitors, or an argument between a husband and wife who are not getting along. You'll find that the parties involved do not recognize or honor the other's values or encourage each other to express their life purpose.

Let's start with values first, because they are the seed from which purpose grows.

Values Are the Heart of the Matter

Your values are what make you tick. Your values are the seat and source of your desires. Yet most people don't really think about their values or the values of others, even when they're considering what it takes to be happy and fulfilled.

Whenever we're speaking to someone about the possibility of coming into business with us, the first thing we do is to discover what his or her values are. In fact, we base our relationships with people on their values and how they relate to us and to ours.

Our values are the wellspring from which comes all that we want in life, everything we seek or search for. Our values are the source of who we think we are. Let's look at an example of a value.

One of the most powerful values many people share today is *belonging*. People want to be part of what's going on and what's happening.

Did you know that there are more than 120 formal twelve-step groups operating in the United States today? People really want to belong, and they often want us to know who they are and what it is they belong to, as well. That's another value, which some marketers are now calling *egonomics*.

Look at the T-shirts, athletic gear, and hats we buy—even if we've never shot a basket, run a mile, or sailed. These items have the brand names of the teams plastered all over them. These products do more than just advertise the manufacturer's name. They are statements of their owners' values.

Look at the license plates on our cars. Ten or fifteen years ago, they were meaningless combinations of letters and numbers. Today they say things like BOBS AUDI, BMW4MOM, and GOLFPRO.

Do you think a man or a woman wearing a Rolex is expressing his or her values? That's pretty straightforward, right? Now, look at this: we know a multimillionaire who wears a forty-eight-dollar Timex because it's an expression of *his* values! He likes people to notice his inexpensive watch—and to know that he could wear anything, no matter how much it costs. One of his values is being different; another is being thrifty.

Values are so intrinsic to who we are that we don't really choose to have them. It's almost as though we are showing what values have chosen us. Values are that compelling.

Values motivate us. When we find that our values not being respected by certain people or institutions, we make those people and institutions disappear, like the stranger in Yossarian's tent in the novel *Catch-22*.

We will not keep company with people who do not honor our values. We will not do business with companies that do not respect the expression of our values.

Let us give you a famous example. Have you ever shopped at Nordstrom? Nordstrom is a very successful department store chain, and one reason it is so successful is that it is very big on honoring people's values. The company plays live piano music in its stores and serves food to shoppers. It bends over backward to have a "the customer is king or queen" image. It is a real and tangible value for each of its current and potential customers.

Nordstrom also has one of the most liberal return policies in all of shoppingdom. One day an elderly woman came in and told a Nordstrom salesman that she wanted to return something that was out in her car. The salesclerk accompanied her to the parking lot and proceeded to unload four tires the woman was dissatisfied with. He promptly wrote up her credit, returned her money, thanked her for her patronage, and expressed the hope that she would return and find her future purchases more satisfactory.

Pretty good service, I'd say: true respect for the customer's values. There's just one thing: Nordstrom has never sold tires! We should mention that we don't know if this story is true. After all, how could the clerk "credit" a payment that was never made or in their system? But we do know this: it is part of Nordstrom lore. And it is repeated from manager to manager, and now even from customer to customer. Nordstrom has become almost synonymous with exemplary service. Here's the point: Respect my values and you've got a friend for life. Ignore them and . . .

What do you suppose is at the heart of the high divorce rate in the United States? What do you suppose would happen to the institution of marriage if all the husbands and wives respected and supported each other's values? Yet how many spouses truly know with clarity what each other's values are?

Values are the bottom line. What are *your* values? What qualities do you most admire and most want to experience and express in your life?

In a moment, we're going to ask you to write down some of your values, but first we want to explain something that might shift the way you see values and help them be more powerfully in your service, if only by making them more specific and more clear for you.

All of our values matter, even the most seemingly superficial ones. However, the real power lies in the values we consider essential. *Essential values* have nothing else inside them; they're like prime numbers, which can't be divided any further. You could also call them *source values*. They are really the heart of the matter.

Let's look at money as an example. Suppose you decide that having money is a value for you. Ask yourself this: "When I have money, what will it bring me?" If you can answer that question with something other than money, then money itself is not an essential value. Look deeper.

You might say that money will bring you a house, a new car, travel, education for your kids, or something else. When you have one of those commodities, what will *that* bring you?

We're asking you to be a bit more serious and even rigorous about asking these questions. Your answers will probably surprise you—and please you, too.

For instance, if you say you want money so you can have a new house, and then you ask, "If I could have that new house, what would that bring me?" you might answer "security for my family," "peace of mind," or "prestige." Now you're getting down to essential stuff, the stuff that dreams and happiness are made of. What's fascinating is that money itself is rarely—perhaps never—a truly essential value. Nobody really wants the Midas touch, but many of us do want freedom, adventure, fun, recognition, appreciation, belonging, independence, creativity, and so forth.

Now make a list of the top five values you have in your life, and keep asking yourself clarifying questions until you have no more answers and have gotten down to the essence of each value.

Value 1 _____

Value 2 _____

Value 3 _____

Value 4 _____

Value 5 _____

More often than not, you won't be able to come up with these values by yourself. You may want to do this exercise with someone else and have him or her ask questions to flush out the essence of your values.

Plato wrote, "The truth is revealed in dialogue." We believe that the truth is revealed through scripture, prayer, and dialogue. Dialogue is an important element.

Peter's business has him talking to lots of people about their values. He doesn't ask right out, "So, Joan, what are your essential values?," because most people wouldn't know how to answer that. Instead, he asks about where Joan lives, what she thinks about and feels, and what (if anything) she'd like to be different in her life. He asks about her family, her work, and what she does for fun, including hobbies.

Sometimes, if Peter is feeling particularly close to the person—and decidedly brave in that moment—he'll ask the most powerful and profound question of all time: "Joan, are you happy?"

Be careful with this one. Some people consider it an intrusion. Others will get so distraught that they will "disappear from view," even though they're still sitting right in front of you. It's not a good question to ask at a party, but if you are sincerely interested in a person, and you really want to know, fast, what's important to him or her, ask it. Then listen.

Two things will happen. First, you will learn things about people that they probably haven't shared with anyone else. You will know these people in a way that is actually closer than the way most of their friends and relatives know them.

Second, you'll probably make some good friends. Here is a story from Richard Brooke, CEO and president of Oxyfresh USA, that illustrates what we mean:

A psychologist once did a research project that required him to fly from New York to Los Angeles. His task was to sit next to another passenger and engage that person in six hours of conversation, never once making a declarative statement about himself. He was only to ask the other person questions.

When the plane landed, the psychologist had a team of his people there in the airport, ready to interview his fellow passenger. What they found was that the man with whom the psychologist had just spent the entire coast-to-coast trip had only two things to say: (1) "That man? The one sitting next to me? Yes—he is the most interesting person I've ever met!" and (2) "His name? Gosh—now that you mention it, I didn't get the fellow's name!"

Ask and you shall receive—all you ever wanted and more. And one of the things you will receive is the key to success in working with other people. Ask them questions that reveal their values—then listen. People love to talk about interesting things, and for most of us, the most interesting thing in the world is *ourselves.*

One more thing about values: they change. Just because you've written a list of your top five values today doesn't mean that new ones won't emerge or that the old ones won't be replaced someday—any day.

If there is one law of life we've learned, it's the fact that everything changes. Your beliefs, your values, and even your purpose, which we'll talk about next, are ever-changing. That's one way you can tell whether you are learning and growing. If you find yourself doing the same-old, same-old for a long time, look out! Change is the nature of things in our universe. Everything around us is changing—and you and I must change, too.

Now let's talk about your life purpose.

Life Purpose

There are two kinds of people in this world: people who are purposeful and people who seem rather purposeless. The difference is that one is living his or her life purpose and the other is not. This is one of those pass-fail, black-and-white matters: either you have a purpose that gets you out of bed in the morning or you don't.

"A man without a purpose," wrote nineteenth-century Scottish writer and historian Thomas Carlyle, "is like a ship without a rudder."

Purpose is not something to be completed or finished, like a goal. You achieve your life purpose by living your life in accordance with the values your purpose experiences and expresses. Purpose is your vision. Purpose calls forth your passion.

Look at people with purpose: Winston Churchill, John F. Kennedy, Golda Meir, Martin Luther King Jr., Thomas Edison, Michael Jordan, Henry Ford, Margaret Thatcher, Ronald Reagan, Mother Teresa, Babe Ruth—the list is endless. These heroes and heroines are from every possible walk of life. They are people with purpose.

We recognize public people of purpose easily, from the arts and sciences, sports, business, politics and government, entertainment, education, and more. But you don't have to be a famous person to live your life in a heroic way. All that's required is having a goal that's bigger than you are. In fact, that's the one key thing about purpose: it's always about making a contribution to others.

Look at the list of people above. All of those men and women have inspired countless others. No matter how egocentric or self-absorbed they may have seemed at any given points in their lives—and it is true that a big sense of self seems to go hand in hand with a big dream—they've all made a difference to people, lots and lots of people. They've had a vision, a goal, and a purpose that was bigger than they were at the time—much bigger. That's the key.

We've all heard stories of people whose vision and purpose drove them on to break through seemingly impossible limitations. Purpose is the driving force in all accomplishments of greatness. But such great achievements are not reserved for public figures who make it into history books or onto *Access Hollywood*. In fact, there are many more ordinary people living extraordinary lives than we will ever know about.

One thing all of these wonderful people have in common is a clear, powerful life purpose. All they have needed is a stage or a playing field to give them the opportunity to live their lives as the high achievers their purpose inspires them to be.

None of these people were born with this purpose already in their minds. You can certainly wait around, being open to the possibilities, and someday your life purpose will probably occur to you. However, if you're excited and you know the awesome power of having a life purpose that brings forth your values and that enables you to experience the rich rewards life has to offer, you might want to take your imaginative birthright and develop a powerful, passionate purpose right now.

How do you do that? You do it the same way you develop beliefs that support you. *You make it up.*

Write down your list of values again, followed by a sentence or two that includes a life purpose that would allow you to experience and express each value to the fullest. Remember that the key is to contribute to others. Be very clear: if your purpose does not include making a big difference in other people's lives, it's off the mark. Remember, too, that the purpose you're going to write down isn't cast in anything unchangeable. In fact, do it in pencil so you can make all the changes you want, whenever you want.

Value 1 _____

_____

_____

Value 2 _____

_____

_____

Value 3 _____

_____

_____

Value 4 _____

_____

_____

Value 5 _____

_____

_____

Your life purpose could be further described as the following:

- The cornerstone of your motivation
- The keystone of your work ethic
- Whatever calls forth your passion
- The standard by which you judge your progress and whether or not you're on or off track
- The big dream in which all your other goals and aspirations play supporting parts
- The reason for your success
- Whatever gets you out of bed in the morning

Like a book, a life purpose may not accurately be judged by its "cover." A person's life purpose may be disarmingly simple. In fact, the most powerful ones usually are.

Peter once had the good fortune to speak with a man who had spent his life working closely with Mother Teresa in her clinic in Calcutta. He was curious about what life purpose lay behind this amazing woman, whose life and work had inspired so many people around the world. So he asked his new friend, and here's what he said: "Mother's purpose is to have people die with smiles on their faces."

"That's it?" Peter thought. Here was one of the most awe-inspiring people in the world, a woman devoted to serving humanity, who gave up everything to work with the lowest outcasts and rejected poor of India, and all her purpose amounted to was having people *die smiling*? It didn't seem right.

So Peter pressed for more details, and the man elaborated. He said that in the poverty-stricken streets where Mother Teresa worked her mission, most people died suffering, in agony, abandoned, and alone. That they should die with smiles on their faces, he said, was the fulfillment of Mother Teresa's work. That's how she knew that through faith and love, she had eased their pain and comforted their lives. Such a simple expression for such a powerful and meaningful purpose.

Service to others is the key to a powerful life purpose. Remember that service brings out the best in all of us. When we are serving others, we really shine.

Think about what your heart is telling you and take a crack at expanding the list you made before. Now write a rough draft of your life purpose on a separate sheet of paper.

Once you've established your purpose, all the other success and happiness principles we're going to explore in this book become easy.

Brad Nelson knew from an early age that he wanted to be a doctor. He grew up watching medical dramas on television, treating his younger brother's cuts and scrapes, and dreaming of the day he'd put on his white lab coat for the first time.

By the time he reached college, Brad's thoughts had taken a different direction. Too often, he skipped his chemistry study group to play touch football with his buddies, and Saturday night keggers were more tempting than studying biology. His medical school applications were rejected with stunning swiftness.

Although becoming a doctor was no longer on the agenda, Brad was still interested in the medical field. After graduation, he took an entry-level job with Middle West Health Partners, a large nonprofit organization that owned several hospitals, urgent-care centers, physician practices, and other health care facilities. It seemed like a good use of his education, and since the company had so many branches, he thought there would be plenty of room for advancement.

He did advance, to some extent, but as the years passed, Brad became increasingly disenchanted with his life at Middle West. As in most organizations of its size, there was a complicated bureaucracy that he found frustrating. It seemed to take forever to get the simplest things approved, and many projects were inexplicably canceled after months of work had already been completed. From time to time, Brad thought about looking for another job, but he made a good salary and the benefits were fine, and now he had a wife and kids to think about. He settled into a middle management position in which five people reported to him and he reported to a whole lot more. It wasn't great, but whose job was, really?

Returning to his college for his twenty-fifth class reunion, Brad caught up with a fraternity brother he'd lost touch with about ten years earlier and was surprised to learn that he'd made a career change. At age forty, Bill had left his job on Wall Street and started a very successful financial planning firm. "It's something I always wanted to do, and I finally decided to take the plunge," Bill said. "It was a little daunting at first, but it's the best thing I've ever done. I've never been happier."

Driving home from the reunion, Brad thought about how energized Bill had become when he talked about his work. Clearly he had found what he was meant to do, and Brad felt a bit envious.

In the weeks after his conversation with Bill, Brad's complacency about his job turned into an unsettling restlessness. For the first time, he allowed himself to really think about what he did all day, and it depressed him. Since he had joined Middle West, the company had grown considerably, but somehow his opportunities for advancement and real job satisfaction seemed to have decreased. Brad realized that he spent more time justifying his department's expenditures than doing long-range planning, and he spent entirely too many hours sitting through meetings that neither involved nor interested him. Even though he had a job in health care, it was far from the career he'd envisioned. It had become little more than a paycheck.

But that paycheck was necessary to support his family of five, so Brad continued plodding through his workdays until a weeklong mission to Haiti brought a welcome relief from his routine. Members of his church had been traveling to the same village for several years, but this was the first time Brad had been able to join them. The experience was eye-opening, to say the least. The poverty was overwhelming, and the people in the village tugged at his heart. Their lives were simple and difficult, but they didn't seem all that unhappy. He guessed it was because this was the only life they'd ever known. Brad eagerly threw himself into helping to add a room onto the tiny medical clinic his fellow parishioners had built on a previous trip. He felt truly useful for the first time in years.

As he put up walls and nailed down floorboards, Brad watched four of his friends go about their work in the next room. A doctor, two nurses, and a dentist, all veterans of these trips, spent long hours tending to patients of all ages, many of whom were brought from neighboring villages by other missionaries. Conditions were diagnosed and treated, children were vaccinated, and mothers were taught how to better meet their families' nutritional needs with what little they had. Lying on his cot each night, Brad marveled at the difference those medical professionals were making in the villagers' health and quality of life. He was glad he could make a small contribution by helping to enlarge the clinic, but it didn't seem like much compared to what the others were doing.

Back at home, Brad couldn't get the trip out of his mind. He talked about it for hours to his wife, Kathy, his children, his parents, his co-workers, and anyone else who would listen. He wanted to go back. He wanted to quit his soul-crushing job, pack up his family, and move to Haiti. He knew it wasn't a practical idea, given the age of his younger children, but he thought about it anyway. At the very least, he wished that he'd studied harder and gone to medical school. He could certainly do more to help people if he were a doctor.

Late one night, after he had spent nearly an hour lamenting aloud, Kathy said, "You know, Brad, you don't have to go all the way to Haiti to find people who need help. You don't even have to leave town, and you certainly don't have to be a doctor. There are plenty of people right here who aren't getting adequate medical care, and sometimes it's just because they fall through the cracks. They're not part of the system, so they become invisible, and they don't know how to change that. If you start looking, I'm sure you could find something satisfying to do a little closer to home."

During the next few days, Brad continued to replay Kathy's comments in his mind, and slowly he began to feel a shift in his thought patterns. Maybe she was right. Why had he wanted to become a doctor in the first place? Thinking back, he realized it hadn't been about the money or the prestige. He'd genuinely wanted to help people who were sick. He'd wanted to relieve suffering, and—who knows?—maybe even save a few lives. Now, even though he technically worked in the health care industry, he wasn't really helping anyone.

He knew that his company's hospitals provided a certain amount of charity care, but it would never be enough, and the people in charge didn't seem anxious to increase their efforts in that area. Their priorities leaned more toward buying a multimillion-dollar robotics system for the surgeons and other expensive, high-tech equipment. Brad knew those kinds of investments were important, but he also knew they formed the basis of enticing marketing campaigns designed to attract more patients—patients whose care was covered by insurance. What about the increasing number of people without insurance? What about the ones who didn't realize charity care was available, or those who were too embarrassed to ask for it, or those who simply gave up after sitting for three hours in an emergency waiting room?

There really were people in his own community who needed help. As he thought about them—who they were, where they lived, what their lives must be like—Brad began to feel something he'd never fully experienced before—a sense of purpose. Perhaps he'd had it back in high school, but it had slipped away in college, allowing him to choose fun over work until all those medical schools had told him he'd thrown away his chances of becoming a doctor. Even on his best days at Middle West, he had never felt a sense of purpose—not like the one that was taking root inside him now.

Maybe his mind-numbing job wasn't a waste after all. It had taught him about the structure of health care in his community. He knew about the services that were available and those that were lacking. He'd learned how the business side of health care worked. And he'd gotten to know people who knew the things he didn't.

Brad didn't know exactly what his future held, but he was beginning to sense that his life was finally taking direction. For now, that was enough. With a little time, he'd figure out the rest.

For more than twenty years, Brad hadn't given much thought to his life's purpose. If someone had asked, he probably would have mentioned being a good husband and father, living his Christian values, maybe something about contributing to the success of the company that issued his paycheck. It wasn't until he began to dig deeper—to peel away the layers of the onion—that he began to get a handle on the real purpose that would drive the rest of his life. When he is finally able to get more specific and start living his purpose, it won't detract from being a good family man, a good Christian, and a good employee. It will enhance those aspects of his life and help him become better at all of them.

We'll catch up with Brad a little later, but first let's talk about a key ingredient he'll need (and so will you) to build a life of significance: imagination.

Fire Up Your Imagination

Logic will get you from A to B. Imagination
will take you everywhere.
—*Albert Einstein*

I f one of the foremost thinkers in history was a proponent
of using your imagination, who are we to argue?

We'll even take Einstein's statement a step further.
Without imagination, it's hard to get anywhere. Imagination is
one of the key ingredients for figuring out where you want to go
and how to get there.

You might not readily associate the word *imagination* with
Einstein, but it's surely hard not to associate it with Walt Disney,
who had one of the greatest imaginations of our time. As early
as the 1940s, as he watched his daughters play on the local
merry-go-round, Disney began to dream about a spotlessly clean,

well-designed amusement park where both children and their parents could enjoy themselves at the same time. After letting the idea percolate for a few years, he got to work, and by July 1955, Disney had turned 160 acres of Southern California orange groves into Disneyland.

It wasn't easy. When he had trouble finding financing, Disney emptied his savings account, sold his vacation home, and borrowed against his life insurance to keep his dream alive. But his vision for his park was so strong and so powerful that he was willing to risk everything he'd built to turn it into a reality. Before any of the now familiar attractions—Frontierland, Fantasyland, Tomorrowland—were constructed or even committed to an artist's sketch pad, they existed in minute detail in Disney's imagination. And when he launched Walt Disney, Inc., the firm that would eventually design and build Disneyland, he called his employees "imagineers," because that was the quality he valued most: imagination.

Walt didn't retire his imagination once Disneyland was completed. When he developed his first television series in 1954, at a time when that medium was still in its infancy, he shot the show in color even though all TV programs were broadcast in black-and-white. Disney had the imagination to envision that someday television would be in color just as films already were, and he'd be ready for it. A short time later, he aired an episode called "Man in Space," using information supplied by a group of scientists, to provide his viewers with a glimpse into the possibilities of space flight. The program even included the concept of landing a man on the moon. That was in 1955. It would be another five years before the U.S. government even began a space program. That's imagination.

By the mid-1960s, Disney was quietly buying up hundreds of acres of cypress-covered swampland in central Florida, because his imagination had conceived an even larger, grander theme park that would include hotels, golf courses, an elaborate transportation system, and much more. In the days before his death in 1966, he lay in his hospital bed, using the tiles on the ceiling as a grid to plan what would become the Epcot theme park at Disney World.

Five years later, at the grand opening of the Walt Disney World Resort in Orlando, a reporter was talking with Ron Miller, Disney's son-in-law, and remarked that it was too bad Walt didn't live to see this.

"He did," Miller replied. "That's why you're looking at it now."

Imagination is a critical faculty—one of the mental exercises that keeps the minds of truly successful, happy people young and fresh. Imagination is one of our greatest and, sad to say, least used resources. For some reason, people assume that imagination is the sole province of artists, children, and crazy people. In *A Midsummer Night's Dream*, William Shakespeare put these words into the mouth of the duke Theseus:

> The lunatic, the lover, and the poet
> Are of imagination all compact:
> One sees more devils than vast hell can hold,
> That is, the madman: the lover, all as frantic,
> Sees Helen's beauty in a brow of Egypt:
> The poet's eye, in a fine frenzy rolling,
> Doth glance from heaven to earth, from earth to
>   heaven;
> And as imagination bodies forth
> The forms of things unknown, the poet's pen
> Turns them to shapes and gives to airy nothing
> A local habitation and a name.

But the duke had it wrong. We all have the gift of the poet, rich in the possibilities of boundless imagination—the ability to give shapes and names to things unknown, to dream. We just forget.

Just as intuition is not only for women, imagination is not only for artists; it's for all of us. For most people, though, imagination is a muscle that's not used enough to be flexible and strong. So take it to the gym and give it a good workout a couple of times a week, and pretty soon your imagination will have biceps like Arnold Schwarzenegger's.

You might think that you have little or no imagination, but that's not the case. The truth is that you use your imagination all the time, even if you're not consciously aware of it. When you decided to paint your living room hunter green rather than the beige color you'd had for a decade, your imagination enabled you to envision a different look for your home. When you threw some tarragon into your favorite chicken recipe, or mixed and matched a couple of chili recipes you found online to get the exact ingredients you wanted, your imagination told you what flavor combinations would appeal to you and your family. Each time you shop for Christmas or birthday gifts, you use your imagination to determine which items would make the recipient's eyes light up.

How do you kick your imagination into high gear so it can begin to open doors for you? Here are a few tips:

- *Be curious.* When you hear or read a word that's unfamiliar to you, look up the meaning. When a news broadcast features a story on a country you're unfamiliar with, head to your computer to learn where it is and a little bit about it. When you're talking with friends or family members, ask questions, especially "Why?" Curiosity is the first cousin of imagination.

- *Associate with creative people who stimulate your mind.* This doesn't require living in SoHo and hobnobbing with sculptors. There are creative people in all walks of life. They're simply people who are interested in the world, who are curious, and who enjoy talking about more than who won last night's game.
- *Hang out with children.* They have the biggest, liveliest imaginations you'll find anywhere. A young child will imagine that dolls can talk, that a lump of clay is really a dog, and that a backyard game of baseball is really the World Series. Ask children questions and let their imaginations fuel your own.
- *Look at everyday objects and think about how they could be improved.* Nothing is perfect; everything evolves. How would you build a better iPad, microwave oven, or belt buckle?
- *Try a creative pursuit like writing a short story, painting, or making pottery.* You don't have to be great or even good. You don't even have to show anyone your work. You're just stretching the muscles of your imagination.
- *Play games like charades and Pictionary.* They stimulate your own imagination while exposing you to the creativity of others.

Should You Be a Daydream Believer?

One way in which you're probably already using your imagination is by daydreaming. Don't be embarrassed; we all do it. When we're driving on a long stretch of highway, clocking off miles on the treadmill, or falling asleep at night, we all engage in a little daydreaming. Although too much daydreaming is clearly counterproductive, a moderate amount can foster creativity and help you focus in on the things that will enable you to build a significant life.

Start paying more attention to your daydreams by taking this short quiz.

In your most recent or most common daydream, what are you doing?

_____

_____

_____

Who are you with?

_____

_____

_____

Where do you live? Describe the setting in detail, including the climate, the type of home or work setting you're in, and even the furnishings.

_____

_____

_____

How do you spend your time?

_____

_____

_____

How do you look? Are you wearing casual clothes, or are you dressed up? Again, be as specific as possible.

_____

_____

_____

What else is significant or noticeable about the life you imagine for yourself?

_____

_____

_____

Consider the possibility that your daydreams, which live in the world in which your imagination meets your conscious mind, are sending you messages about what you really want from your life. Are you listening to those messages? Are you taking action on them?

One way to make productive use of your daydreams is to turn them into visualizations. We'll talk more about this in chapter 7, but let's get started now.

Creative visualization is the process of affecting events simply by directing your own thoughts, and it's all about imagination. It's often used by athletes who are working to improve their performance, but it's equally effective for anyone seeking to improve his or her life, so it should definitely be in your toolbox for building a significant life. No equipment is necessary.

There are many excellent books on visualization techniques, but here's a quick overview. First, determine the goal you want to work toward—the more specific, the better. It can be a professional goal such as reaching a million dollars in sales, a personal goal such as losing twenty pounds so you look great on your upcoming beach vacation, or an overall image of the life you'd like to be living. (Don't know what your goal is yet? Don't worry, we'll get to that soon.)

Next, clear some time when you can be alone for a few minutes and get into a comfortable position. Focus for a minute or two on your breathing and on getting rid of any tension in your body.

Now use your imagination to visualize, in as much detail as possible, what it is you'd like to achieve. Use all five senses—sight, sound, touch, smell, and taste—to put yourself physically into your ideal scene. Maybe you're in a comfortable family room with the spouse and children you hope to have someday. Maybe you're in a well-appointed corner office, having been promoted to vice president of your company. Maybe you're retired, living comfortably in a quiet beachfront community surrounded by friends and family members.

The key to success is to make your visualizations as detailed as possible. Feel the fabric of the chair you're sitting on. Hear the voices of the people in your life. Smell the sea air or the scent of your favorite meal in the oven. Really get into the scene with as much clarity as possible.

That's how athletes do it. A basketball player who is trying to perfect his free-throw technique feels the ball in his hand. He sees the hoop in front of him—the exact height and distance it would be if he were actually standing on the gym floor. He hears the noise from the fans. He smells the combination of scents in the arena, from sweat to food vendors. He tastes the cold water he just sipped on the sidelines and the hard rubber of his mouth guard. Then he uses his imagination to make the perfect shot over and over again.

The more you practice visualization, the more skilled you'll become at it and the more clarity you'll be able to achieve. You'll find many opportunities to work it into your daily life. When you're stuck in a traffic jam, close your eyes for just a few seconds and visualize your goal. Take a moment when you're brushing your teeth, when you're making dinner, or when you're eating lunch in your office. We think you'll be surprised at the results.

The writer George Bernard Shaw was a believer. He said, "Imagination is the beginning of creation. You imagine what you desire, you will what you imagine, and at last you create what you will." In just two sentences Shaw sums up the power of both imagination and desire. Wow.

Maria Hinostroza sighed heavily as she helped Mr. Goldman back into his hospital bed, adjusted the height, raised the side railing, and locked it into place. It was nearly 8 P.M. and she was tired, although her shift didn't end for another three hours. Maybe some coffee would help.

Entering the small break room, Maria made an effort to look away from the leftover sheet cake on the counter. Today was the tenth anniversary of the day her friend Karla began working at Pinewood Heights, an assisted living facility in a Chicago suburb. The staff of the rehabilitation wing had a cake for every occasion: birthdays, employment anniversaries, and holidays. Maria had gained twelve pounds since she started working here. She didn't need any more cake.

Maria had been thrilled when she'd gotten the job as a nurse's aide. In the years since her family had emigrated from Peru, she'd finished high school, then worked in fast-food chains and grocery stores before her cousin Yolanda had recommended her for this job. Yolanda had said she'd be lucky to get the job, and she was right. The pay wasn't great, but it was better than what Maria had been making, and she received medical benefits.

At first, she had loved the job. She was a quick learner, she was popular with the patients and staff alike, and the second shift seemed to suit her. She enjoyed having free time during the day, although she didn't do much with it.

After three years, however, she was feeling restless. Dressing and bathing patients, helping them to and from the bathroom, and making beds had become mindless tasks she could do by rote. Maybe she wasn't physically tired as much as she was just plain bored, she thought as she returned to the floor.

Maria sighed again as she entered the room of Mrs. Bonner, preparing to take her vital signs.

"Oh, I'm sorry. Didn't mean to interrupt," Maria said quickly as she noticed Janet Henry, the facility's nurse practitioner, who was talking with Mrs. Bonner.

"No problem, Maria," Janet said with a smile. "I'm just finishing up and about to be on my way." She turned back to Mrs. Bonner and continued, "Okay, then, I'm going to start reducing those medications that we talked about. If everything keeps improving, I think you'll be on your way home in a few days."

Maria stepped aside to let Janet leave the room. She was in awe of Janet. They were about the same age and they worked in the same place, but their jobs couldn't be more different. Although Maria enjoyed the patient contact and was proud of her role in helping them, she was keenly aware that the tasks she performed each day paled in comparison to what Janet did. As a nurse practitioner, she outranked even the registered nurses. She ordered tests and interpreted them. She decided who needed physical therapy, and who needed an EKG, and who was ready to be released. With some limitations, she was even licensed to prescribe medications. To Maria, she seemed almost like a doctor.

Maria had been watching Janet for a few months now, and she harbored a secret desire to be just like her. But since she had only a high school education, that seemed impossible. She'd done some research and knew that she'd need years of school, years full of science and math—impossible.

Over lunch the next day, Maria's mother, Isabel, said, "You've been quiet lately. Is something wrong?"

"No, I'm okay. Just a little—I don't know, bored, I guess? I like my job, but it's gotten to be the same thing every day, and it doesn't feel like enough."

"You're lucky to have such a good job," her mother chided. "A lot of people would be very happy with what you have. Imagine if we were back in Peru. What would you have then? Not a good job like this, I can tell you that."

"I know, and I don't mean to be ungrateful," Maria replied. "It's just that all those years you talked about leaving Peru and coming to the United States, you used to tell us that if we lived here, we could do anything we wanted, *be* anything we wanted. And I guess sometimes I just wish that were really true."

"What is it that you want to be?"

"I'd like to be a nurse."

"But you *are* a nurse."

"No, Mama, I'm a nurse's *aide*. That's an entirely different thing. Nurses—the real ones—have so much more responsibility, and they really get to help the patients. I do little things to help, and what I do is important, but I wish I could do more. There's a woman at work who's a nurse practitioner, which is kind of like a supernurse. She can even prescribe medicine for patients, almost like a doctor."

"So why don't you do that? You're a smart girl."

Maria laughed. "It's not quite that simple. I only went to high school. To be a nurse practitioner, you have to go to college for four years to get a nursing degree, then go even more to get a master's degree. It's a lot of years and a lot of work."

"You're a hard worker."

"Yeah, but it's also a lot of money and—I don't know, it's just a lot. I'm fine doing what I'm doing."

Isabel looked at her daughter and frowned. "You know what your problem is, Maria? You've got no imagination."

"What?" Maria laughed. "What does that have to do with anything?"

"Ever since I was a teenager, I dreamed about coming to the United States. I read books about it, and every time I met someone who had been here, I asked them a hundred questions about what it was like. After I married your father, I put it into the back of my mind because I was busy with you and your sister, but after your father died, I started thinking about it again. I thought about it all the time, imagining what it would be like to live here and have you girls grow up in this country."

"That's just daydreaming, Mama. Daydreaming doesn't make anything true."

"We're here, aren't we?"

"Well, yes, we're here, but not because you daydreamed about coming here."

"Maybe not directly, but it's part of the reason. Everybody thought I was crazy to think that I could move to another country with two young children and no husband, but I knew it was possible. I'd lie in bed at night, after you girls were asleep, and picture exactly what our life would be like. I saw a small apartment with a bedroom for me and one for you girls. I saw myself going to work every day and shopping at the grocery and speaking English to everyone I saw. I saw it in such detail, it was like a movie playing in my head."

"I still don't see the connection."

"I spent so much time picturing us here, in our American home, that I started to believe it could really happen, and all of a sudden I found myself thinking of ways to do it. I talked about it to everyone I could find, hoping someone would have contacts here who could help. I even got a job at the American embassy to meet more people and learn more, and I tried to speak English at home as much as I could. After a while, the doors started opening up, and now here we are. Do you remember the first apartment we lived in? It looked almost exactly like the one I kept picturing before I went to sleep at night. It was like I'd imagined it into reality."

"So you're saying that's what I need to do? Imagine myself being a nurse like Janet, and then I'll be one?"

"I'm saying that it wouldn't hurt. If you give up before you've even started, you'll never be anything more than you are, but if you use your imagination, I'm sure you can find a way to make it happen."

"Maybe you're right," Maria said. "I'll think about it."

She did think about it, and thought some more. Maria bought a book on visualization and started practicing for a few minutes each day. At first her mind wandered and she got frustrated, but in time the process became easier and she found herself conjuring up an increasingly clear picture of herself, still working at Pinewood but now as a full-fledged nurse practitioner. She saw herself in the kind of scrubs that Janet wore, and she even imagined that the two of them were friends, chatting over lunch in the tiny break room.

Her mother was right. The more Maria visualized herself in that role, the more she felt comfortable that it fit her, and the more it emboldened her to think about how she might begin to pursue it.

Late one afternoon, Maria was in the break room at Pinewood, sipping her coffee, when Janet walked in.

"Maria! I'm glad I ran into you," she said.

"Oh, do you need some help with a patient?" Maria responded, starting to get up from her chair.

"No, nothing like that. I'm on the board at Fisk Career Academy, and we've just gotten clearance to expand the nursing program there. I don't know if you're interested, but I've seen how good you are with the patients here, and I think you'd make a great nurse. If you'd like, I could help you put your application together and set you up with the financial aid office. It's a part-time program, so you could continue to work here, but you'll need to move quickly because the new spots will fill up fast."

Maria stared in dumbstruck silence.

"Maria? Are you okay?"

"Yes! Sorry, I'm fine, just a little—surprised. I've actually been trying to work up the nerve to ask you for advice about going to nursing school. I'd love to do what you do."

"Well, that's a happy coincidence, then," Janet replied. "Are you working tomorrow? Maybe we can start on your application then."

"That would be great," Maria said. "Thank you so much." She turned and made herself busy pouring another cup of coffee so Janet wouldn't see the tears welling up in her eyes as she pictured her mother, all those years ago, sitting in a cramped house in Peru and picturing herself and her daughters living in the United States. Her mother's imagination had transported the three of them nearly four thousand miles. Now Maria was starting her own journey. She wondered how far it would take her.

Of course, it takes more than an active, creative imagination to build a life of significance. The trick is to channel your imagination into productive goals, but first we should address something that could derail you before you've even begun: fear.

Don't Fear to Be Fearless

Nothing in life is to be feared. It is only
to be understood.
—*Marie Curie*

Fear is a difficult subject to tackle head-on but an easy one to overcome. To get a handle on fear, let's speak for a moment on the matter of belief.

Belief is the key to success and significance. No matter what career or business enterprise you choose, you must believe in what you are doing. You must believe in your company, its mission, its integrity, and what it stands for, and you must believe in the people you work with as well. In your personal life, belief is equally essential—belief in your family and the principles by which you live your life.

There's no way to fake any of this. If you don't believe in what you're doing, you simply cannot be either successful or happy.

We've all met businesspeople whose words just didn't ring true—like a Honda salesperson who drives a Toyota. How many people do you know who are trading their time for money in a job they can't stand? How persuasive, honest, and service-oriented is a person who doesn't believe in what he or she is doing for work, much less to make a living? How many people do you know who are living deeply unhappy personal lives because they are behaving in ways that run counter to their basic beliefs?

Belief, like life purpose, is one of those pass-fail things. Either you have it or you don't. You must believe in your values, unique talents and special gifts, purpose, goals, dreams, and aspirations. You must know that what you are doing is making a difference, that you and your efforts are making a real contribution to others. After all, if *you* don't believe in yourself and in what you're doing, who will?

Everything Is Sales

Belief is the key to successful sales. Every business, career, occupation, and enterprise of any kind is about sales. In fact, every interaction you have with all of the people you come in contact with each day in your personal life involves sales.

Many people don't want to hear that *everything* is sales. That's because most people are in the habit of saying (or thinking), "I can't sell," "I don't like to sell or be sold anything," and "I won't sell." (How's that for no possibility?)

Perhaps that's why we pay salespeople so much. They're the Green Berets of business: "It's a dirty job—but *somebody* has to do it." Since nobody wants to sell, it's obviously one of the most dangerous and risky jobs around, so those high income–earning salespeople must be getting hazard pay!

Just for fun, next time you meet someone who says he doesn't like or want to sell, ask him to tell you more about that. Then sit back and listen as he spends the next five minutes or more masterfully selling you on how he can't sell.

Everything is sales.

We sell our friends on going with us to the movie we want to see, the restaurant where we want to eat, and the dessert we want to share. We sell our kids on believing in themselves and on cleaning up their rooms. We sell ideas, concepts, thoughts, opinions, and feelings. Teachers sell knowledge and discovery. When we first met our spouses, we sold them on the idea that we were worth dating and eventually marrying.

But the most important sale of the day is what we sell to ourselves.

When people say they can't sell, it's simply not the truth. What they are really saying is, "I don't believe I can sell. I don't believe in myself." And you know what? That's just not true, either! They believe, all right: they have a *negative* belief about sales and a negative belief about themselves. And every negative belief, no matter how artfully conceived or rationally explained, comes down to being one big, nearly universal, negative belief that every single person on the planet shares: fear.

Fear: Friend or Foe?

The enemy of a powerful belief is fear. Fear is what hurts us, because it stops us in the successful pursuit of our goals and purpose. Fear is what each of us must learn to conquer.

There are schools of philosophy that say, "Love your fears." That doesn't make much sense to us. We all have fear. Some of it's healthy, too. But love it? We'd rather lose it.

Let's make a distinction here. It's good to have some fears, such as being afraid to step in front of a speeding truck. We should be afraid of things like chainsaws and other power tools, guns, cars going 120 miles per hour, 220 volts of electricity, tornadoes, drunk drivers, war, and things like that. Those are pretty healthy fears. They compel us to act with great respect and to take care when crossing the street, sawing logs, or repairing an appliance. Those fears motivate us to take positive action. It would be foolish to be fearless in those and many other situations.

What examples do you have of fears that strengthen you, keep you aware, and support you in your life and your work?

The point is that fear in itself isn't good or bad. Just like beliefs, fear can be either healthy or unhealthy. Fear is a tool, and as with any tool that can be used to build or to destroy, the quality of how it serves you or undermines your efforts is up to you. It's just another choice.

In most situations (other than crossing the freeway, rewiring your home, and other life-threatening ones), choosing fear means choosing a life of unfulfilled goals and aspirations. This choice is the true enemy of happiness.

Fear of What?

The most common fear we human beings have is fear of the unknown. For some reason, we got it into our collective minds ages ago that we had to know what would happen before we took action. "Safety first" was drummed into us until it became fear of the unknown. Although this is the most common fear of all—probably the source of that other monster fear, the fear of dying—the following story may serve to rid you of this fear once and for all.

A man was convicted of treason and sentenced to death by firing squad. As the drums rolled, the man faced his executioners. The commanding general announced, "Sir, you have a choice: you can accept your fate and die before this firing squad, or you can go through that black door over there."

He was given two hours to think about it.

Two hours later, the man was returned to the prison yard, placed in front of the firing squad, his hands bound, and a blindfold placed over his eyes. The general then asked him, "What have you chosen?"

The man replied, "I have no idea what I might face behind that black door. It could be a most terrible fate. I choose the firing squad."

The order was given and shots rang out. The man fell to the ground, dead.

As the gunmen were leaving the prison, one turned to the general and asked, "Sir, what was behind that door?"

The general, without expression, replied, "Freedom."

Risky Business

Fear of the unknown comes from the desire to avoid risk. Very often, risk means anxiety. Did you know that the Chinese character that represents crisis is made up of two smaller characters? One means "risk" and the other means "opportunity." To reduce anxiety, people avoid the unknown.

Facing the unknown means accepting the challenge of the unknown, and to accept that challenge, we must have self-discipline and belief.

Have you ever seen a James Bond movie? Secret agent 007 has a tendency to walk right into his enemy's stronghold and confront the sinister villain (Goldfinger, Dr. No, and the others) face-to-face. It's great! Bond has no idea what's going to happen, but you can be sure that if he messes up, it's going to be *horrible*. One time he was going to be fed to the sharks; another time, cut in half with a laser. But no matter—he always gets out of it. He keeps his cool. He is disciplined. He believes in himself—even when he has no idea what's coming next.

For too many people, self-discipline literally means self-punishment. What do we do with an out-of-control twelve-year-old boy headed for what used to be called juvenile delinquency? We send him to military school for some discipline—and that's punishment.

Discipline, however, comes from the word *disciple*, which means two very interesting things: a "follower" and a "learner." Discipline comes from following and learning from someone or something. Self-discipline comes from learning about and following one's own beliefs.

People who follow their limiting beliefs by avoiding learning about the unknown are actually very disciplined. They never take chances. You see, discipline can be either strengthening or limiting. When you're following a positive belief and purpose, discipline is actually a freeing and powerful concept, not a limiting one.

Discipline is something we can all cultivate. A good synonym for discipline is *integrity*. It's as simple as doing what you say you're going to do—keeping your word. You can do that, especially with yourself, only when your belief is bigger than your fears.

There's another aspect of fear of the unknown that most people don't consider, and that's the fear of simply *looking at things differently*. We get so stuck in what we think we know and the sameness of things, yet the safety of that prevents us from even considering something new. It's a security that prohibits us from looking out beyond that old tried-and-true position or point of view, and it's a major stumbling block to coming up with new and better ways of doing things.

Below you see a pattern of nine dots. Here's what we want you to do:

Connect all nine dots using only four straight lines and without raising your pen or pencil from the page. You can crisscross lines, but you can't lift the pen from the page.

Got it? Okay, now do it.

How did you do?

If by some chance your mind was a bit stuck in the same-old, same-old way of looking at things, here's the key to finding the answer: you've got to get outside the nine dots. How do you do that? See page 85 for the solution.

Now, if you're really stuck in a pattern of limited thinking, you're saying to yourself, "That's cheating."

But it isn't at all. The solution follows the directions exactly. It just backs up a bit and takes a bigger picture of what's possible. It reaches into the unknown—going beyond what you think you know and even beyond what you think you don't know into the realm of what *you don't know* that you don't know. The fascinating fact is that this is the place of greatest possibilities for your success and happiness.

Live and work like an artist with a blank canvas. Be willing to risk the inevitable "failures" that going beyond your experience presents. That's where all the real rewards are. After all, if you keep doing things the way you've been doing them, you're bound to end up with what you've already got.

The reason most people aren't willing to do this is a fear of failure.

"To Fail or Not to Fail?": What a Question!

The next fear to conquer is the fear of failure, and the surest way to do that is to change your understanding of the value of what we usually call failure.

One of America's true high achievers, Thomas Edison, had this to say about failure: "To double your success rate, you must double your failure rate."

Author Zig Ziglar has said that if you close only one out of twenty-five sales calls, each failure is simply one step closer to making the next sale.

Do you know that failures are critical to success? There is not a successful man or woman on earth who was not a major failure many times before attaining the mantle of success.

A very wealthy businessman once began a speech by saying, "It's true that I am successful, probably the most successful person in this room. Would you like to know why? It is because I have failed more times than anyone here."

Check out the impressive track record of another famous success story:

- Fired from his job in 1832
- Defeated for state legislature in 1832
- Declared bankruptcy in 1833

- Elected to state legislature in 1834
- Lost his sweetheart to death in 1835
- Had a nervous breakdown in 1836
- Defeated for Speaker of the state legislature in 1838
- Defeated in nomination for Congress in 1843
- Elected to Congress in 1846
- Lost bid for renomination in 1848
- Rejected for job as land officer in 1849
- Defeated for Senate in 1854
- Defeated for nomination for vice president in 1856
- Defeated for Senate a second time in 1858
- Elected president of the United States in 1860

Abraham Lincoln is certainly not remembered today for the many defeats and failures in his life.

The two greatest home run hitters in the history of baseball are Barry Bonds and Hank Aaron. Did you know that Hank struck out 1,383 times during his career and that Barry struck out 1,539 times? And we can't forget the Babe. Babe Ruth will most likely be remembered as the greatest home run hitter ever. Know how many times he struck out? 1,330.

Do you understand now what the wealthy businessman above is saying?

Thomas Edison had a dream of making a working electric incandescent lightbulb. Yet time after time, his experiments failed. After about the hundredth time, one of his frustrated young associates said to him, "Can't you see that this isn't destined to work, that you're not going to succeed? You've failed one hundred times already!"

Edison replied, "I have not failed at all. I have successfully determined one hundred ways that it will not work; therefore, I'm one hundred ways closer to the one way it *will* work."

Failure and success are just two more things we make up. To Edison's assistant, the great inventor had failed a hundred times. But to Edison himself, he had succeeded a hundred times in learning what *not* to do.

Is it helpful for you to define or describe yourself as a failure? Perhaps you think that if you fail often enough, you'll get to a point where you just can't stand it anymore and you'll start succeeding. That's called *backward motivation.* Why not start right now by acknowledging your successes instead?

Here's a great exercise: list ten successes you've had today in the spaces provided below. Even if you're reading this just after you've awakened early in the morning and you don't think you've done anything successful yet, think again, then list ten successes you've already had today.

1. _____
2. _____
3. _____
4. _____
5. _____
6. _____
7. _____
8. _____
9. _____
10. _____

How did you do? Did you have trouble listing ten successes? If you did, that's a clue that the way you define things is not serving you and not encouraging you. You still think it works to pile up failures until there's no more room for them and you'll just *have* to succeed.

Did you get out of bed this morning? That's a success. Did you shower, shave, or brush your teeth? Did you pray? Those are successes. What else did you do today? That's a success; that's a success; that's a success!

You *must* get into the habit of defining your actions and the results that occur in your life and work as successful. Honestly—that's all success is. It's a habit. And like any other habit you have, you learn it by repetition. You do it over and over and over and over, until it's something you do without thinking.

You made a habit of tying your shoes. You don't think about *how* you do it anymore; you just do it. At first you had to do that whole "Rabbit runs around the tree and down through the hole" business, but after a while, tying your shoes stopped being a rabbit and started being a habit. It takes no thought; you just do it.

Success (or failure) is just the same. If you set a task for yourself that every evening before you go to sleep you will list (in writing) ten successes—or twenty-five or fifty, if you're impatient and want the crash course—then very soon you will establish the habit of success.

Can you imagine a better habit to have? I guarantee you can do this. It's easy and fun—and it works!

We call these ingrained, habitual attitudes *habitudes*. This is the habitude you need to have if you want to avoid failure, disappointment, poverty, and loneliness.

We want to stress that *failure* and *poverty* do not mean the same thing. For the sake of this book, we're assuming that most people desire financial success along with all the other successes of a richly rewarding life. After all, in this Western culture of ours, you're going to require money to achieve many of the goals you've set for yourself. In a very real sense, money is required for freedom in today's world. But there are many poor people who are not failures—and many rich ones who are!

The *fear* of poverty, however, has the same root as the fear of failure.

Poverty and wealth are diametrically opposed. If you don't want poverty, you simply must stay away from it—on all levels, not just financial. There's emotional poverty, social poverty, intellectual poverty, and more, just as there is abundance in all these areas. Avoiding these poverties may sound difficult to do, but as we said earlier, one of the few things over which you have true and total control is your thoughts—and remember, your thoughts can ultimately shape your reality. We want to be clear here. This is not a book about the "law of attraction." We absolutely do not believe in blaming the victim. Those who suffer from horrible diseases or are victims of crime are not to be blamed. The victims of the tsunami in Asia or the earthquake in Haiti did not bring it in themselves by their thoughts. Sometimes, bad things happen. This is not meant to be a theological work. We are simply saying that we have more control than most of us think.

Your thoughts are something you can choose. In fact, it's with our thoughts that we have the God-given power of choice. Once again, you must have the discipline and the focus to keep all of your positive thoughts in your mind while removing all negative thoughts.

Have you ever tried to kick out a negative thought? (The word *try* is in itself a clue that you're on the wrong track.) It's like taking a stray animal, feeding it for a couple of weeks, and then deciding you don't want it around anymore. The animal will still keep coming back again and again. It's not easy to get rid of negative thoughts, no matter how unwanted they may be. In fact, lots of times it's nearly impossible. That's why so many people pay good money for courses and products to help them *try* to stop smoking, lose weight, and get rid of any other prevalent bad habit.

Instead, what you must do is simply replace the limiting thought with a positive one. Each time that a limiting thought or fear starts to replay in your mind, stop the thought right in midsentence and replace it with its opposite—a positive thought.

Your thoughts not only often become your reality, they also determine your feelings, and the emotional energy of feeling is a powerful ally for shaping either success or failure. Again, it's a choice, and it's up to each of us, moment by moment, to make the choice for success and happiness.

That's another really important point: the business of developing positive thoughts is a moment-by-moment thing. The instant you succeed in turning a negative to a positive, that negative is going to do its best to reassert itself. After all, it's fighting for its life! But then, so are you—and it is really all up to you which of the two wins.

What State Do You Live In?

No, this is not an inquiry about your geographical location. What is your state *of mind*?

All fears, including the most destructive fears of poverty and failure, are nothing more than states of mind.

States of mind come about by the mental habits we choose over and over until they exist automatically. When we are in a given state of mind, we've probably just found ourselves there without really knowing how we got there or why. We don't plan the trip. We just show up in Doubtville or Can't City or wherever.

This is important, because these states of mind can cause our results, and they can absolutely cause the most negative and most disastrous results. So developing the states of mind that serve and give power to your goals and purpose is a very

75

important skill to learn. It takes discipline: learning and following our positive beliefs.

Fortunately, there is a wonderful built-in mechanism that will help you tremendously: the conscious mind can hold only one thought at a time. This is a real blessing. It makes it so much easier to remove a negative thought if you can replace it immediately with a positive thought.

How do you do that? Do you remember when Julie Andrews sang "My Favorite Things" in *The Sound of Music*? Whether it's raindrops on roses, Christmas, ice cream, having a nurturing relationship, learning to play the guitar, or learning to speak Italian, that's what you can use to replace any and all negative thoughts.

See yourself doing what you've always wanted to do. In your mind, picture yourself having achieved your dreams and desires: sailing the ocean, speaking to eight hundred people and inspiring them all, or traveling to Nepal. The minute a negative thought pops into your mind, slap the success disc of your life into the DVD player of your mind. Keep playing it again and again until it's the state of mind you normally walk around in.

Now you're living in a great state!

TIPS FROM PETER

One of the first things I learned to do to shift my state of mind was the exercise of tallying up each day's successes. Soon, not only was I increasing my habit of success but another thing I didn't expect also began to happen: I began to realize how grateful I was.

Really—I began building the habit of gratitude as well as the habit of success. Believe me, if you want to walk around in a powerful state of mind that will have you on top of the world, bringing you great results you never dreamed were possible, gratitude is it.

Now I regularly replace negative states with grateful states simply by listing all the things in my life I'm grateful for. I start saying them to myself one by one: I'm thankful for my wonderful family, for my many friends (and I list them each by name). I can go on forever. The sun, this day, the clouds, the rain, the flowers, my car, the speedometer, numbers, lights, windshields—see how the list of things you're grateful for just builds and grows? The result is instant smiles! It's a great state of mind, and it's so powerful!

Fear carries with it the danger of paralyzing you and completely stifling your actions; even more important, fear kills inspiration and imagination. *Fears* of failure obviously lead to *beliefs* of failure; fears of poverty lead to beliefs of poverty. Fears encourage procrastination, kill ambition, and invite unhappiness in every form. We're convinced that many illnesses, even organic disorders, can be healed by replacing the limiting fears in our minds with powerful beliefs.

The way to conquer fearful thoughts is to strongly insist that they leave. The subconscious mind will believe anything you tell it. Develop states of mind that support and encourage you.

The Critic

There's one more fear we need to discuss: the fear of criticism. This commonly manifests as "What will others think of me?" We call it the fear of not looking good.

How we look to others is one of the most powerful motivators of human behavior. There's nothing wrong with looking good. Everyone likes to look good, and we're sure you do, too. But when we sacrifice our integrity to look good, when we lie—by commission or omission—to protect our public image, we undermine our goals and purpose and champion beliefs of fear and failure.

Shakespeare had this fear—and its antidote—pegged perfectly when he wrote, "This above all: To thine own self be true."

The number-one reason that people try to steal our dreams—and that's what a great deal of criticism comes down to—is that our dreams force other people to take responsibility for themselves. Our dreams compel other people to admit to themselves that they, too, are in control of their lives. Our own dreams force others to take responsibility for where they are today and where they will be tomorrow.

When you take a stand, you're going to catch some flak from people who haven't the courage that you have. It comes with the territory. *Courage* means "heart" and "being on purpose." The changes we are talking about here require courage. The true warrior is one who has the courage to do battle with the enemies within oneself.

Which do you think comes first: having courage and then taking action, or taking action and then drawing courage from it?

Let's let Henry Ford answer this one: "Courage follows action."

Don't be surprised by people's desperate fear of criticism. After all, for many centuries human beings have been punished and even killed for having the courage to express beliefs that were different from those held by the majority: Galileo, Joan of Arc, Martin Luther King Jr., and many more. We have a horrible intolerance for new and different beliefs that threaten the status quo.

Nonetheless, we must resist this fear with all our might. The fear of criticism leads to indecision, and it is the primary reason for a lack of ambition, motivation, and purpose.

President Theodore Roosevelt said the following:

It is not the critic who counts—not the man who points out how the strong man stumbled or where the doer could have done better. The credit belongs to the man who is actually in the arena, whose face is marred by dust and sweat and blood. Who strives valiantly, who errs and comes short again and again, who knows the great enthusiasms, the great devotions, and spends himself in a worthy cause. . . . Who, at the least knows, in the end, the triumph of high achievement, and who, at the worst, if he fails, at least fails while doing greatly, so that his place shall never be with those cold and timid souls who know neither victory nor defeat.

We can be thankful together for the fact that we have the power to overcome and conquer the fear of criticism and all other fears.

Once you give it a try, you might find that it's actually fun to be a warrior in this battle with your fears. At first you might not be very good at it, just as in sports or any other new pursuit, but you'll be surprised at how quickly you'll improve and how good you'll become. It doesn't take long. And since you've already learned to embrace a challenge, something else will happen: you'll start looking for bigger fears to battle. That's the problem with this business of conquering fear: once you start doing it, there are fewer fears left to fight anymore! Once that happens, we need to move on to even more exciting and fulfilling challenges.

In the weeks following Brad Nelson's epiphany, he found that he was often preoccupied. Now, however, his thoughts had shifted from the Haitian village to his own city and how he could fulfill his newfound mission. He knew that he wanted to turn his health care background into a way to make a real difference in the lives of others. Of that he was certain. Beyond that, he hadn't a clue.

Going about his workday, as he walked through the corridors of Middle West's hospitals and office buildings, he began to pay more attention to his surroundings, hoping inspiration would strike. Who was falling through the cracks? Who wasn't being served adequately? How could the organization make changes that would begin to fill those gaps? And how could he, a respected employee but one pretty low in the pecking order, find a way to make that happen?

It didn't take long for him to find the answer to the last question: he couldn't. If there was one thing he knew about Middle West Health Partners, it was that the wheels moved slowly, if at all, when it came to making major changes. The board of directors had decided more than three years ago to tear down two outdated office buildings and replace them with a new tower that would house an ambulatory care clinic and physician offices. The wrecking ball had yet to arrive. In order to make anything happen, Brad would have to leave his job and start a new company, where he would call the shots. The idea thrilled him, but he still didn't know how to begin.

Remembering the old adage that knowledge is power, Brad ate a quick lunch at his desk and headed for a bookstore near his office. He was a frequent customer there, but usually his mission was to pick up a few magazines on cars and auto racing or the latest volume in the fantasy fiction series his daughter loved. On this day, he found his way to the business section, and it was overwhelming. There were multiple rows of books on every topic imaginable, and two rows specifically on starting and managing your own business. Wow, there was a lot to learn.

Forty-five minutes later, Brad headed back to his car. His credit card had taken a hit, but he was armed with a shopping bag filled with books and magazines he hoped would help him start to figure this out.

Later that night, Brad passed up a basketball game on television to dive into his research. He headed into the room left vacant when his son, Jon, had left for college, and stretched out on the bed, surrounded by his purchases from the bookstore. It didn't take long for his enthusiasm to wane a bit. *How* many new businesses fail within the first year? Really? After about an hour, he stacked the books on the floor next to the bed and got up. Maybe he could still catch the last half of the game.

The next week, as Brad continued to educate himself on the ins and outs of entrepreneurship, he felt his enthusiasm slowly being replaced by doubts. How would he finance a business of his own? His credit rating was fine, but would a bank risk money on someone who was unproven? He and Kathy certainly didn't have the means to provide the financing themselves. They had one child in college and two more heading there in a few years. Kathy was a stay-at-home mom. They were stretched thin already.

That Saturday night, after their children were in bed, Brad and Kathy sat down to watch television, settling on a movie that followed the lives of seven friends who attended college together. A few minutes later, Kathy nudged him playfully and said, "That guy Eric reminds me a little of you at that age."

As the show continued, Brad began to see the resemblance. The character of Eric was a life-of-the-party kind of guy who came from three generations of lawyers, and his family assumed he'd be the fourth. Eric, however, was beginning to realize that law school simply wasn't in his future and was struggling with the prospect of breaking that news to his family.

The story took Brad back to his own college days. When he'd begun the process of applying to medical schools, his adviser had pointedly told him that he was a long shot for acceptance. "Your test scores are adequate, but your grades are well below what they should be, and you don't have the extracurriculars to make up for them," she'd said. "I wouldn't get my hopes up."

The conversation had come as a blow. Obviously, Brad had known his grades could have been better, but each semester he'd convinced himself that he had more time. Nevertheless, he completed his applications—three to universities with stellar programs and two more to lower-ranked schools that he considered backups—and put the process out of his mind.

Within a few weeks, the first rejection letter had come, followed quickly by four more. Even his own university, the one that was about to confer a bachelor's degree on him, didn't want him in its medical program. There would be no Dr. Brad Nelson. He'd failed at the one thing he'd wanted to do his entire life, and there was no one to blame but himself.

After the movie's closing credits rolled, Brad had trouble shaking the slight disconcerting feeling the film had given him. It had been a long time since he'd really thought about his aborted medical career. After he'd gotten the job at Middle West and he and Kathy had started their family, he'd been too busy to think about it, and that chapter of his life had gradually faded into the background. Now, remembering how he'd felt when those rejection letters had come, he began to have doubts about his chances of success in whatever new venture he might undertake. He had failed then. It could happen again, and now that he had a family, the stakes were a lot higher this time.

Brad went to bed feeling vaguely unsettled, and the feeling stayed with him for the next few days. At the office, he rededicated himself to his job and pushed aside the idea of leaving. His boss was nearing retirement age. Maybe if he worked harder, he'd be considered for a promotion. At least it would mean more money and a change of pace.

Kathy noticed that Brad had stopped talking about starting his own business. When she casually asked about it, he gave a vague reply about needing to give it more thought and changed the subject. A few days before Jon was scheduled to arrive home from college for the summer, she moved Brad's business books out of their son's room, putting them back in the bag from the bookstore and leaving it in a corner of the family room. Brad didn't seem to notice.

Jon arrived on a Saturday, and the following day he and Brad sat down to watch a baseball game on TV. During a commercial break, Jon said, "So Dad, since I've been home, I've been so busy filling you in on everything I've been doing at school that I haven't had a chance to ask about you. A few weeks ago, you were telling me on the phone that you were thinking about starting your own business. How's that going?"

Brad shifted uneasily in his chair and hesitated before responding. "I don't know. I haven't thought much more about it, to tell you the truth."

"Really? That surprises me, because you sounded so excited about the idea. What happened?"

"Nothing, I guess. I think I went off half-cocked, as my dad would say, and didn't really think it through. I'm not sure it's such a good idea."

Jon paused for a moment, then continued to push. It wasn't like his father to be so tentative and evasive. "Why wouldn't it be a good idea? I think you'd be great at running your own show."

For several minutes, Brad rambled vaguely about some of the issues he'd encountered when he'd begun researching the idea of launching a business. He talked about the difficulties of getting financing, the need for a detailed business plan, the pitfalls of hiring and keeping good employees. "And those are just a handful of the million and one things that could potentially go wrong," he said.

"Let me get this straight. You're afraid you're going to fail, so you're not going to chance it? You're not even going to try?" Jon asked.

"Well, I wouldn't put it that way," Brad replied, sounding a bit defensive.

"I would," Jon said. "Look, Dad, you and I have been bonding over baseball for as long as I can remember. Did you ever think about the fact that our favorite sport is the one with the highest failure rate? The best hitters in the league fail nearly 70 percent of the time, but they keep stepping up to the plate and trying again. Why can't you do that? It's what you'd tell me to do, right?"

"I see your point," Brad said with a laugh. "At least I wouldn't be striking out in front of thousands of fans."

"Exactly!" Jon replied. "My economics professor talked a little about that stuff last semester. One day we had a guest speaker—a guy who runs a venture capital company that loans money to start-up businesses. He said he'd be reluctant to lend money to an entrepreneur who hadn't had at least one failed business, because failing taught them so much. It helped them learn what not to do the next time, kind of like a batter learning what pitches not to swing at. He said he admired them because they had the guts to come back from failure and try again. It sounded weird at the time, but I guess it makes sense."

"Yeah, I guess it does. Hey, base hit!" Brad said, as the action on the television screen caught his attention again. The two men settled back to continue watching the game, but Brad had begun to feel something shift deep inside. He idly wondered where Kathy had put those books he'd bought.

No one wants to fail, but failure is simply part of life. The real failure comes when we let our fears paralyze us and keep us from moving forward. If we let that happen, how will we ever find success? Brad knows he still has a long road ahead and is likely to face many challenges as he continues the journey he's begun. But he's ready to put his fears aside and step out into the unknown.

We'll check in with him one more time, but for now, we're ready to move forward as well, toward the next key to unlocking your significant life: focus.

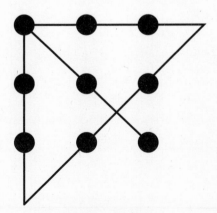

Nine Dots Solution

Sharpen Your Focus

Focus: point at which an object must be situated
so that a well-defined image of it may be produced.
In Latin, it means "fireplace" or "hearth."
—*The Oxford Dictionary of English Etymology*

T he smallest bit of action separates the high achievers and people who find true happiness and fulfillment from everyone else.

The difference between the gold medal and second or third place in an Olympic swimming event is often measured in only hundredths of a second.

How much better is the .300-plus hitter with a multimillion-dollar big-league baseball contract than a second-string, .265 benchwarmer? One to two hits a week over the course of the season is all that makes the difference.

The winner of a major golf tournament like the Masters often wins by one stroke—a difference for the four-day tournament of less than 0.4 percent better than the runner-up.

These examples are all from the world of athletic competition, but they are indicative of the tiny-bit-better-than performance percentage that separates the winners from the losers in any field of endeavor: sports, business, relationships, you name it.

The difference between success and failure is actually marginal—measured in a fraction of a percent *at most*. What is it that makes this difference? What quality does the winner have more of than the runner-up or the loser, the person for whom happiness continues to be elusive? Let's answer that with another story.

A master archer was in the forest with two students. As both students were notching their arrows, preparing to shoot at a target off in the distance, the teacher interrupted them and asked each one to describe what he saw.

The first archer said, "I see the sky and the clouds above, I see the fields and grass beyond. I see the different trees of the forest—oak, beech, pine, poplar, and maple—and I see their branches. I see the leaves. I see the target with its colored rings. I see—" The teacher stopped him midsentence and said, "Put down your bow, my son. You are not ready to shoot today."

He then asked the second archer, "What do you see?"

The student replied, "Nothing save the goal at the center of the target, Teacher."

"Then let your arrow fly," the teacher directed. And it did— dead-on to the very center of the target.

The difference between the two students' states of mind was a matter of *single-minded focus*.

And the Blind Saw Anew

We want you to do a demonstration of focus with that we learned from Og Mandino, one of the most inspirational writers and speakers of our time. He has written, among many other titles, *The Greatest Salesman in the World,* a book that has sold more than twenty million copies in at least a dozen languages.

In one of Mandino's speaking presentations, he asks someone from the audience who requires reading glasses to come up and join him on stage. The person removes his or her glasses and attempts to read a page from the newspaper. Of course, it's impossible for that person to see the words.

Then Og (people refer to him as Og) hands him a white three-by-five-inch card with a tiny pinhole in the center. That's what we want you to do, even if your vision is clear. Make a white card with a pinhole in the middle and look through it at a page of small type—what designers call "mice-type"—that is difficult for you to read or see clearly. Hold the card out in front of you a couple of inches from your eye and move the page of copy back and forth until it comes into focus.

The fascinating thing is this: almost anyone, no matter how poor his or her eyesight is, will be able to read every word through that tiny hole. The type will appear as clear for you as if you had perfect twenty-twenty vision.

The reason is *focus.* That little hole causes your eye to focus. It cuts out all the extra stuff you don't really need to see, bringing all the power of your vision to bear on a small focused point, which dramatically increases your ability to see the letters and words. That's what a pinpointed focus can do in any aspect of your life.

When you learn the ability to focus on anything about yourself, you will master that thing itself. Focus your thoughts and master your mind. Focus your emotions and master your heart. Accomplishing all of this will have you being a master of possibilities, a master of life.

Mastering your mind is the key. Once we train our focus sharply on our goals and desires, our minds act like heat-seeking missiles, leading us through all the lessons we need to learn, through all the trials, tribulations, and celebrations necessary for us to arrive at precisely where we want to be. This is true for as long as we maintain our focus. Yet most people don't maintain their focus. Why not?

Let's do a little experiment. Read over the following statement. Do it quickly and read it just one time.

Finished files are the result of years of scientific study combined with the experience of many years of experts.

Now read it again and count the number of *F*s in the text. Give yourself fifteen to twenty seconds to do this. How many do you see? Three? Four? More?

If your answer was three or four, go back and reread the statement, but this time, look for the number of times you encounter the word *of*.

There are actually seven *F*s in that statement, but in a typical group of people who've never seen this demonstration before, most notice only three *F*s. They don't focus on the *letters* in the statement. What gets in the way of their ability to focus, even with clear and specific directions and even with very straightforward black-and-white information, is that something disables or distracts their focus.

Most of us learned to read phonetically—and *of* appears as "ov" in our "mind's ear." Because we learned to read that way, because we all tend to read by speaking the words aloud in our heads, because we are creatures of habit, because we make assumptions about nearly everything in our lives, and because we lack real and true focus uninterrupted by our constant self-talk chatter, interpretations, meanings, opinions, judgments, and editorializing, we don't see what's staring us in the face. We miss the correct number of *F*s.

This is truly an in-your-face lesson; it's not necessarily polite or kind, it's the kind of wake-up call we all need now and then.

None of us have any hope of success unless we can honestly and truly focus our attention on the task at hand—whatever that task may be. There is much unlearning, much baggage, and much habit that we must discard, replace, or refine before we can approach mastery of the life skill of focus.

Just for fun, here's another one. Read the following familiar passage quickly:

> Mary
>> had a
>> a little lamb

Did you catch that one? We bet you did.

After doing this dozens of times on a flip chart up in front of a room full of people, we can tell you that 80 percent of the time people don't see the double *a*. The reason you saw it now was probably that you were more attentive and focused because of the previous exercise. That just shows you how easy it is to keep a keen edge on your focusing ability. Like everything else, all it takes is a little practice.

Synergy: $2 + 2 = 1,640,209$

One powerful way to stay in focus is to use a principle described by Napoleon Hill in his masterpiece of success literature, *Think and Grow Rich*: the concept of the Mastermind group. Hill describes his Mastermind group as "the coordination of knowledge and effort, in a spirit of harmony, between two or more people, for the attainment of a definite purpose."

It's vital that you find a group of peers—we suggest between four and six, including yourself—with whom you can discuss all of your challenges, seek solutions to your problems, and figure out how to optimize your opportunities. You will find that five minds together have the sum total of much more than those five minds. They are the equivalent of one supermind.

The mechanism at work here was best explained by a man with one of the most astonishing minds the world has ever encountered: the American engineer Buckminster Fuller. If ever there was a model of empowering beliefs, universal values, extraordinary purpose, and every other quality we're writing about here, including focus, it's Dr. Fuller.

He created a scientific explanation of the principle of synergy, the ability of something to be greater than the sum of all of its individual parts. Fuller realized that relationships themselves have a certain magic that can transform each individual ingredient, making the whole even more powerful than the mere number of its parts would indicate was possible.

He created a formula for the synergy of a group of people together that goes like this: $P^2 - P \div 2 = S$. This means that the number of people (P) squared, minus the number of people and divided by two, equals the number of synergistic relationships (S) present in the group.

Following Fuller's formula, if you have 100 people in a room, squaring that would be 10,000; minus the number of people, 100, equals 9,900; divided by two would be 4,950. So in a group of 100 people, there are actually 4,950 relationships in the room.

If you've ever wondered how a church service, a workshop, or an opportunity meeting can be so powerful and exciting, this is why. There aren't simply 100 people there. There are 4,950 relationships. And if all of those relationships are equally engaged in the same uplifting possibility, the lid can come off that room with ease.

We recommend that you have four to six people in your Mastermind group because synergy kicks in with four or more people.

Using the synergy formula, if you have only three people, that's 3 squared equals 9, minus 3 equals 6, divided by 2 equals 3. But look what happens with just one more person: 4 squared equals 16, minus 4 equals 12, divided by 2 equals 6—six relationships in a group of four people, two more relationships than there are people present. How can that be?

Just look carefully at the numbers. Draw a line connecting all the relationships in the hexagon of six dots below.

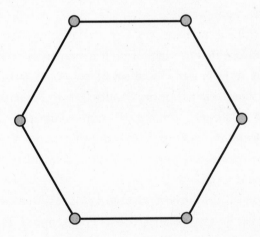

You should have fifteen lines when you've finished (see page 107 for the solution). This corresponds exactly with Fuller's equation: 6 squared equals 36, minus 6 equals 30, divided by 2 equals 15. As you can see, the key here is the relationships, not simply the number of people present. That's the power of the Mastermind group: synergy.

TIPS FROM PETER

I learned from reading Napoleon Hill's book that the people who make up my Mastermind group don't all have to be in my current circle of friends. He taught me that I could imagine and create my own Mastermind group with people I'd never met or who weren't even living anymore. What a fantastic way to learn and benefit from the greatest hearts and minds in history!

Of course, you first must truly be familiar with the men and women you're choosing, in the words of Napoleon Hill, as your "invisible counselors." This includes reading their biographies and autobiographies and studying their lives and their works so you become very comfortable with your beliefs about how these people would solve problems and create new opportunities.

Just for a moment, close your eyes and imagine sitting around a conference table with the men and women of your choice. At Hill's table there sat Ralph Waldo Emerson, Thomas Paine, Thomas Edison, Charles Darwin, Abraham Lincoln, Luther Burbank (American horticulturalist), Napoleon Bonaparte, Henry Ford, and Andrew Carnegie. Choose your counselors as carefully as Hill did; surround yourself with greatness.

Around my Mastermind table sit Moses, Ayn Rand, Napoleon Hill, Robin Williams, Joe Namath, and J. K. Rowling. Here at my mind's table I sit, surrounded by greatness, and we discuss any question or concern I pose.

During one particular Mastermind meeting late last year, I asked my group a question. At this point we had been meeting together for more than six months on a weekly basis, so we were already very comfortable with one another. The question I posed was, "What must I do

94

to increase my earnings by 20 percent within the next six months?"

All of us thought for a while; Moses was the one who came up with the answer first. The group already knew of my commitment to high achievement, but Moses gave an answer that added a powerful new dimension. Here's what he said:

> Not only must you be committed to yourself and your beliefs, you also must be committed to other people's beliefs even more than you are committed to yourself. You must be focused on empowering others to achieve their goals and aspirations.

For the next two months, I worked only with people who were already involved in my relationship marketing organization to help them succeed. I changed the game, achieving my goal in two months instead of six!

Two of my people reached levels of success and wealth that before they had only dared dreamed was possible, and in the same period, my earnings not only increased the 20 percent I'd envisioned—they doubled!

Thank you, Moses!

The issues we discuss aren't always business-related. My Masterminds have helped me move closer to many of my personal goals, deepen my friendships, and bring more fun into my life. Choose your Mastermind group well, bearing in mind your life purpose and the goals we'll be working on in the next chapter, and you'll be amazed at how they can help you bring things into focus.

I also found it interesting that over time I had begun to take on some of the dominant characteristics of each member of my Mastermind group. Why not learn from the best?

As you just read, Moses has given me a broader view of the road to significance, where all my goals and efforts grew to include serving and empowering others. Moses taught me leadership.

I can be an exceedingly serious person sometimes, and Robin Williams's influence has allowed me to see the humor in everything, to approach life and work more playfully. I am never more alive than when I am caught up fully in laughing.

From Napoleon Hill, I've seen the awesome power that comes from coupling intelligence with an even stronger dose of self-generated optimism; Hill's my attitude coach.

Ayn Rand helped me to realize that mediocrity is a curse and that it is immoral to give less than everything you have. She opened my eyes to living a truly passionate life.

Joe Namath, the great New York Jets quarterback, has taught me how to keep my eye on the ball. If you've ever seen Namath play, you've had a masterful show-and-tell of the power of focus. With the power of his focus, Joe controlled twenty-two pro football players, their entire teams, the sixty thousand people in the stands, and the hundreds of thousands watching on TV.

J. K. Rowling, the British author who created the beloved Harry Potter series, showed me how to find beauty in everything life offers. When she conceived Harry Potter and his magical life at Hogwarts, she was unemployed and living on welfare, yet it was during this difficult time that she made magic in her own life and introduced a beautiful, magical world to millions of children and adults alike.

What the Mastermind group does, besides generating a ton of creative solutions and new possibilities, is to help optimize your focusing power. By making focusing a formal affair, you begin to retrain your consciousness, imagination, and creative intelligence to generate your goals and desires. Focus is simply a matter of practice.

_____

Your Mastermind Group

Now it's time to form your own Mastermind group. Write down the names of the people you'll be consulting with, along with your reasons for including them—the specific qualities they'll bring to the table.

1. _____
_____
_____

2. _____
_____
_____

3. _____
_____
_____

4. _____
_____
_____

5. _____
_____
_____

6. _____
_____
_____

Whose Mind Is It, Anyway?

What do you do when you have a negative, nonsupportive thought?

What many of us do is focus on it, get wrapped up in it, and become enraptured by it, as though we were going to make love to it—and that's a big mistake, because thoughts breed like rabbits. What we get when we entertain those negative thoughts is just more of the same.

For example, suppose you start thinking about finances, and the next moment, your wonderfully imaginative mind washes over you like a stormy sea with wave after wave of negative, depressing, sad, no-possibility junk. Most of us never separate these thoughts from ourselves, which makes *us* negative, bad news, worthless, and all the rest.

Be very clear about this: you are not your mind. Good thoughts, bad thoughts, whatever—you are not those thoughts. Thoughts are something you *have*—like the way you have fingers and toes—not something you *are*. The connection between your thinking and who you are is that the results you cause in your life over time are the product of your habits of thought.

Once you learn to focus your mind, the experience changes: those bogeyperson thoughts come up, and you notice they are there, but you focus instead on what you *want* to be thinking about, and the limiting thoughts simply disappear—at least, for a moment. Chances are, they'll be right back, holding on for dear life.

When that happens, focus again on what you choose to have in mind. Keep doing it and doing it. Sometimes the back-and-forth wrestling match will seem endless. But it will end, and it will actually do so faster than you would ever expect. The mind is very teachable. That is its true nature.

Simply focus on what you choose to think, feel, say, and do. That's the key to shaping your own mind. What's more, there is no other way to live happily with passion. Without focus, life really is a hard road—and a hopeless one. In fact, that's a good definition of hopelessness: the inability to focus on your goals and dreams.

How do you acquire focus? Again, you do it the same way you get to Carnegie Hall: practice, practice, practice.

As with the archers we talked about earlier, single-minded focus on a goal is the way it's done. If you have many different goals, then you may need to practice shifting your focus from target to target. That's okay. Take it one at a time. There are some people who can stay focused on many projects at once, but that doesn't work for most people. Single-minded focus is a skill all successful high achievers have developed.

The place to start is with your mind. Be aware of your thoughts. Inspiring thoughts can stay. Limiting thoughts should be asked to leave. Do this any way that works for you. Shoot the thoughts you want gone. Say "Stop!" Slash them to little pieces with a sword. Coax or sweet-talk them into going away as you would a little child who finds him- or herself in the wrong place at the wrong time. Whatever style is yours and you are comfortable with and good at, use it—as long as it works. Just stop the negative thought. Then replace it with something you choose to think about.

There are some people you just don't want in your home, right? So you don't let them in. If they're already inside, you ask them to leave. This is the same thing. Kick the thoughts you don't want out of your mind. Whether you do it like a diplomat or like a six-foot-six bouncer is up to you. Just make sure they're gone. Your mind is your castle. It's up to you to have around you the kind of thoughts you want to hang out with.

The more you encourage inspiring thoughts to take the place of unwanted thoughts, the easier and more naturally the inspiring thoughts will become predominant in your mind. Practice, practice, practice. That's all there is to it.

Affirmations—written, thought, spoken aloud, or listened to—are powerful allies in this focus-training process. Think of the kinds of thoughts you most want to think and write them on three-by-five-inch cards. Read them every morning and before you go to bed every night. Make a recording of the kinds of positive thoughts, beliefs, attitudes, and habits of thought you want to have and listen to it over and over again.

This may sound hokey to you. If that empowers you, let it be hokey or corny or whatever—but it works. We don't know one high achiever who hasn't used written or taped affirmations in his or her quest for success. It's a proven, powerful tool.

An issue of *Success* magazine profiled the network marketing industry. The feature article began with the story of Richard Brooke, CEO of one of the leading companies in the industry. Brooke's picture was on the cover of the magazine as well.

What readers of that issue didn't know was that a decade earlier, when Brooke was far less well-known (and not the CEO of anything), he had a designer friend of his create a mock-up of the cover of *Success* with his picture on it. He framed it and looked at it every day for ten years. It was a powerful tool he used to help him focus on his success.

Kathy Nelson listened with slight amusement as her husband talked. She loved the animation in his voice and the broad hand gestures he made when he was excited about something. His restless dissatisfaction after the trip to Haiti now had been transformed into boundless energy once he'd discovered his purpose and decided to step out of his comfort zone and take his career in a more satisfying direction.

Tonight he was telling her about a company that manufactured some kind of surgical supplies. Kathy wasn't entirely clear about what the devices were used for, but she listened as Brad described the business and its owner, with whom he'd had lunch earlier that day. The owner wanted to expand the business and was looking for a partner to buy into the company.

"So that's about it," Brad said. "I have a good feeling about this guy, and it sounds like the business has a lot of potential. I need to look into it a little more, but I think we should consider it. What do you think?"

"I guess it sounds fine," Kathy replied. "Obviously I don't know much about surgical supplies, but if the company seems solid, and the price is within the range the bank said we could borrow, I guess we should consider it. But what about that other business you were talking about a couple of days ago? The start-up idea you and Phil had. Something about bar coding."

"Oh, I'm still thinking about that, too. It's just that this one kind of fell into my lap. I don't know. There are just so many possibilities."

Kathy looked at him for a moment, then spoke carefully. "Brad, I love seeing how fired up you are about going out on your own. I think it's great, and I hope you know that I'll support you 100 percent, whatever you end up deciding. I'm just a little concerned about . . ."

"About what?" Brad asked.

"You're all over the place," Kathy continued. "In the past three months, you've had, what, five or six different ideas about businesses you could start and businesses you could buy?

You get really enthusiastic about one thing, then something else pops up that sounds good, and you change direction again. I definitely don't think you should grab the first thing that comes along, but I'm not sure this scattershot approach is working. It's been months since we started talking about this, and it just doesn't seem like we've made any progress. I'm worried that you're going to run out of steam and stay stuck in your old job, and I don't want to see that happen."

"I see what you're saying. There are just so many possibilities, and I keep getting distracted and chasing after the next idea. It's kind of exhausting, to tell you the truth," Brad said with a smile.

"Hey, do you remember two summers ago when we took the kids to Disneyland?" Kathy asked.

"Sure. That was a great trip. A long drive, but fun."

"This reminds me of that trip a little bit."

"Okay, I'm not getting the connection."

"Remember how we spent one day in the park, then visited your brother in San Diego for a few days, and went back for another day at the park before we came home? I'm thinking about how different that second day was because we figured out how to focus."

Brad smiled. He did remember.

They'd arrived at the gates early in the morning on the first day, and the kids were on fire with excitement. They eagerly looked at the map of the park, and Jackie shouted, "I want to go on the Matterhorn!" at the same moment that Hunter yelled, "Splash Mountain!"

"Don't worry," Brad said. "We'll get to all of it. First the Matterhorn, then Splash Mountain."

Although the Matterhorn attraction was in the back of the park, they were full of energy, and no one minded the long walk. By the time they got there, the line was long, but it was worth the wait. An hour later, the family left that area and crossed the park to ride Splash Mountain. After that, they headed for Star Tours near the park entrance, then back to the other side for the Haunted Mansion.

By late afternoon, they were exhausted. Brad had lost track of how many times they'd crisscrossed the large park only to find seemingly endless lines at every attraction. The day was almost over, and they'd been on only a handful of rides. They'd even had to stand in line for half an hour when they stopped at noon for lunch. Everyone was tired and cranky, and the pool at their hotel sounded far more inviting than walking to the back of the park again for It's a Small World. They had planned to return to the park for a final day before driving home, but no one seemed very enthusiastic about it at that point.

Over dinner at his brother's house the next night, Brad recounted how their much-anticipated day at Disneyland had turned into a frustrating disappointment. As he described the experience, his sister-in-law, Becky, laughed and said, "That happened to us when we first moved here. We figured out pretty quickly that planning is the key. You'd be amazed at what a difference it makes if you focus your energy on one thing at a time."

The next day, as the two families sat together on the beach, Becky reached into her bag and brought out a well-worn Disneyland guidebook, a notepad, and a pen. She handed them to Kathy and said, "Come on, I'll give you the tricks of the trade."

Becky proved to be an expert. She explained that most visitors enter the park and automatically go to the right, so early in the day the lines tend to be shorter for the attractions on the left. She knew where the crowds headed immediately after the afternoon parade and how to find the shortest lines at that time of day. She even knew the best times to eat lunch. Within an hour, she'd helped Kathy devise a plan that would enable the family to make the most of its final day in the park. The day turned out to be one of the most fun and memorable times they'd ever had together.

"Okay, I see what you mean," Brad said. "I've been doing the equivalent of crisscrossing Disneyland without focusing on what I really want to do and coming up with a cohesive plan for making it happen."

"I think so," Kathy replied. "Finding our focus worked for us on that trip. Maybe that's what you need to do now. By the way, don't forget that you need to take Jackie to the soup kitchen tomorrow. It's her Girl Scout troop's day to work there."

The next day, Brad was sitting in a corner of the city's largest homeless shelter, engrossed in a book as he waited for his daughter to finish her two-hour shift, when a man approached him.

"I'm Father Bell, director of the shelter. May I help you with something, sir?"

"Oh no, thanks, I'm fine. Just waiting for my daughter. She's with the Girl Scout troop that's helping serve lunch today."

"Okay, then," Father Bell said. "We really appreciate those girls, by the way. We need all the hands we can get, and they're really hard workers."

"Well, not so much when it's time to do dishes at home." Brad was distracted by the sound of coughing. He turned to see a girl about Jackie's age. "That doesn't sound good," he said.

"That's Maya," Father Bell replied. "She came in a few days ago with her parents. She's getting over a pretty bad case of pneumonia."

"Do you have a doctor on staff for things like that?"

"No, we have a nurse who comes in a couple of days a week, but that's it. She's the one who suggested that we take Maya to the emergency room. The poor kid had to sit there for nearly four hours before anyone could see her, but once she got on antibiotics she improved pretty quickly. In a way, it was lucky that she got sick because it turned out that she was behind on her immunizations, so we were able to get that done at the hospital."

At home later that night, Kathy noticed that Brad seemed preoccupied. "Is something on your mind?" she asked.

"Yeah, I was thinking about being at the shelter with Jackie today. That place is doing fabulous work, but they have so many needs. It reminded me of those people back in Haiti. It was their needs that got me started on this journey to find a way to make a difference. I feel like I've gotten away from that initial goal a little bit."

"I guess you're right," Kathy said thoughtfully. "You started out wanting to build clinics and now you're talking about selling surgical supplies."

"Exactly," Brad said.

Late the next Monday afternoon, Brad tapped on the doorway of the head of Middle West's legal department. "Kurt, do you have a second?" he asked.

"Sure, Brad, what can I do for you?"

"I was wondering how hard it is to set up a nonprofit corporation."

"Do you want the long answer or the short one?"

Brad laughed. "The right one, please."

"Are you finished for the day? Let's go have a beer, and you can tell me what you've got in mind."

Over their drinks, Brad briefly described his Haiti trip and subsequent quest to find a way to make a difference in people's lives, ending with his brief discussion with Father Bell the previous Saturday.

"I've been thinking about it, and I think there's a need to take health care directly to the homeless. God knows they're struggling to get it anywhere else."

Kurt listened with interest as Brad outlined an ambitious plan. He envisioned a mobile clinic—a large vehicle stocked with diagnostic equipment, a laboratory, everything needed to bring basic medical services to those who could not or would not seek care through traditional venues. The clinic would travel to shelters, soup kitchens, and parts of the city where homeless people were known to gather. He'd staff it with doctors and nurses—volunteers, at first, until he could afford to hire a staff. Eventually the clinic would begin serving other people who lacked medical services—the city's poorest neighborhoods, public housing complexes—but first he'd focus on the homeless. There would be opportunities to expand later, after he'd gotten things off the ground.

"Other communities are doing this, so I don't see why we can't do it here," Brad said. "I've got a lot of ideas for getting funding, and I'm sure we can get the hospitals to donate some supplies. You and I both know how much stuff they waste every day."

"How long have you been thinking about this?" Kurt asked.

"Honestly? Just since Saturday. My thoughts had been so scattered for the past few months, but all of a sudden it all came into focus and I knew what I wanted. I spent all day yesterday making notes."

"Well, I really like it," Kurt said. "To be honest with you, I wouldn't mind getting involved in something like that myself. I'll be happy to take care of the legal work and anything else I can do to help. Want another beer?"

"Thanks, but I think I'd better get home. I need to tell my wife that I've finally figured out what I want to do when I grow up."

Focus works. If you're running haphazardly through your life, dabbling here and there, maybe it's time to sharpen your vision. Like Brad, once you start to focus, you might find that the answer is right in front of your eyes.

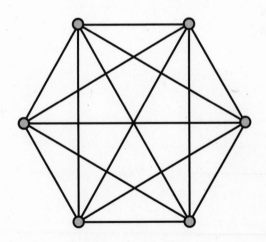

Hexagon Solution

Set Specific Goals

The purpose of goals is to focus our attention.
The mind will not reach toward achievement until
it has clear objectives. The magic begins when we set goals.
It is then that the switch is turned on, the current begins
to flow, and the power to accomplish becomes a reality.
—*from* The Best of Success, *compiled by Wynn Davis*

Do you remember what you were doing when you were fifteen? If someone had asked you at that age (and it's quite likely that someone did—at least, a high school guidance counselor!), "What do you want to do with your life?," do you have any idea what your answer would have been?

If someone asked you that today, do you know what your answer would be?

Do you have an answer? You must! Otherwise you wouldn't be reading this book. The question really is, are you consciously and specifically *aware* of what that answer is?

In 1940, when John Goddard was fifteen years old, he answered that question quite specifically. In fact, he wrote down all the goals he had for his life. He wanted to do the following:

- Run a mile in five minutes or less
- Climb Mount Everest
- Live with indigenous people in Sudan
- Visit all the countries of the world
- Read both the Bible and the *Encyclopedia Britannica* from cover to cover
- Play Claude Debussy's "Clair de Lune" on the piano
- Pilot a submarine
- Write a book

In fact, there were 127 entries on his list of goals!

Today, at age eighty-six, John Goddard is one of the most respected and well-known explorers in the world. He has achieved 108 of his original 127 goals. He has visited 113 countries and intends to visit the rest. He continues to pursue all the goals he has yet to fulfill: exploring the entire length of the Yangtze River in China, walking on the moon, and many, many more exciting adventures.

Such is the power of goals. Where does this power come from, and how can you use it to inspire success for yourself and others? The great New York Yankees philosopher Yogi Berra once said, "If you don't know where you are going, you might wind up someplace else."

Goals and Fellowship

Your life and work can be either a Sunday drive or a purposeful, by-design journey to your true destination: your destiny. *Destination* and *destiny* come from the same Latin word that means to "establish" or "make fast and firm."

That's what goals are all about. They focus us; they make our desires firm and fast. Goals establish the direction for your attention and awareness; they give your imagination a laserlike pointedness and focus your entire arsenal of inspirational tools on the task of turning your dreams into reality.

There is one more thing to consider before we get into goal-setting: you can't *start* with goals. If you skipped straight to this chapter, go back to the beginning, and especially focus on chapter 2. You must start with your purpose. The reason most goal-setting programs fail is that they're not linked to a purpose the person cares about. A goal without a worthwhile purpose to back it up is like a New Year's resolution that gets abandoned by February. What's going to make you do it when the going gets tough? What's the overriding purpose that your goals are linked to?

TIPS FROM PETER

At one of my Mastermind group meetings, I asked the members to tell me more about goals. All eyes went immediately to Napoleon Hill, and we all burst out laughing, because everyone knew that he was the Master of goal-setting and goal-getting in the group, having taught millions his success principles, which are as true today as when he penned them so many decades ago.

Napoleon leaned forward, looked me straight in the eyes, and said, "Peter, if you want to win, if you want success in any endeavor, there is one and only one quality you will require—definiteness of purpose; you must have the knowledge of what you want and a burning desire to possess it.

"You know," he continued, "our world has a habit of making way for anyone whose words and actions show that he knows exactly where he is going."

"Goals," I echoed, as Napoleon nodded.

"So, Peter," he asked me, "where are you going?"

"Are you asking what my goals are?" I countered.

"Yes, but only the ones sizzling in the pan; only the goals with a burning desire standing under them."

(*Standing under*, I thought. Aha! *Understanding*. What a wonderful insight! I love this group!)

So I told him. I flipped open my notebook and read to him from my list of goals. Here are some, from a list of more than a thousand I've written down.

- My first book will be published in the winter of 1994.
- I will be the greatest inspirational speaker in the world.
- I will deliver a talk at Harvard University
- I will deliver a talk at Oxford University.
- I will deliver a talk at Congress.
- I will deliver a talk at the United Nations General Assembly.
- I will deliver a talk at Hebrew University.
- I will speak in Tokyo.
- I will speak in Carnegie Hall.
- I will learn and become fluent in Japanese.

- I will learn and become fluent in Spanish.
- I will learn to play the piano.
- I will learn to ballroom dance.
- I will learn to fly jets.
- I will bicycle along the Great Wall of China.
- I will visit Russia.
- I will visit Eastern Europe.
- I will visit outer space.
- I will own a home in Jerusalem.
- I will work out six days a week for thirty minutes each day.
- I will attend the Super Bowl five years in a row.
- I will write a great horror novel.
- I will buy my wife a gift every month.
- I will take my wife on a date one night a week.
- I will be a radical giver and teach others to do the same.
- I will do everything I do with passion as best I can.
- Every day I will walk closer to God than the previous day.

When I finished reading and looked up, Napoleon and the rest of my group applauded vigorously, shouting "Bravo! Bravo!" I blushed in response, not because I am shy about my goals, but simply because whenever you share your goals with others—or others share their goals with you—there is a power about it. Our goals inspire people.

Goals are very special that way. That's because goals inspire power. They have a life of their own, and when you share them with the right people, those people tap into your goals and get their own infectious energy from them. Right then and there you've involved another person with inspirational and encouraging power to join you in partnership for the accomplishment of your goals.

We should warn you right up front: the chances are good that you'll encounter people who react negatively to your goals. They'll shake their heads and do their "grave dancing" routine. They'll talk "no possibility" to you. But don't ever let that throw you off-track. They are just people who have trouble being in the presence of real courage, determination, and desire. The truth is that your goals scare them.

Do you know why many other people don't have goals? There are four reasons:

1. *They have not been sold on one idea.* This is because they have no belief that they can achieve their goals. We'll talk about the importance of belief later.

2. *They don't know how to set goals.* It's what we call a technical problem; they truly don't know how to set and get their goals.

3. *They are afraid, because setting goals involves risk.* What if they don't get what they want? They're afraid to fail. We've already tackled that one.

4. *Because they lack self-esteem and a positive self-image, they don't think they deserve success and happiness.* They don't deserve success? They don't deserve happiness? This is the saddest reason of all. Of course they deserve success and happiness! Everybody does.

If you've ever participated in one of the hundreds of personal development or personal growth seminars out there, you may have heard a workshop leader say something like, "We're not going to fix anyone here. There is nothing to fix. Get off the thought that you're broken."

Well, we're here to tell you that if you think for one moment that you do not deserve success, happiness, and fulfillment, then something most definitely *is* broken! You do indeed require fixing.

It may be acceptable to some people to walk around with the thought that they don't really deserve to succeed or be happy, but not to us! As far as we're concerned, you *must* be successful, happy, and fulfilled, and that's all there is to it. There is no excuse for not living and working with a level of joy and accomplishment equal to or even beyond your wildest dreams.

If you're not living a significant life, then you are not living!

The time in which we live has been called the Age of Responsibility. We agree; furthermore, that means that it's also the Age of Freedom, because freedom and responsibility are two seemingly opposite but actually complementary sides of the same coin. If you're up for making a better world, if your life purpose has something to do with making a difference to people, with taking a stand for the highest possible quality of life—for yourself and for all the others with whom you come in contact— then *your success* is the most important and powerful contribution you can make.

Your success will have a bigger impact than you can imagine. You can be the one who breaks the logjam of mediocrity that enslaves our world and who propels us all into a future of indescribable beauty, productivity, and joy. Let us explain what we mean by that.

In the areas of Canada where they do the majority of North America's logging, loggers use rivers rather than roads as their highways, floating the huge logs they cut down the river to the sawmills. Sooner or later, the logs get stuck in what we know as a logjam.

The interesting part is that although the loggers are faced with hundreds, even thousands of these great trees tangled up in a hopeless, immovable traffic jam, they know that moving just one log the right way will free up the entire mess and send all those trees floating freely down the river again. They call this one log the *kingpin*.

Is it possible that you are a kingpin? What would happen to the people around you if you were freed up to become a big success? Don't you think that it would inspire and encourage them? We can promise you it would. We cannot count the number of times we've watched organizations and groups of people experience a breakthrough in performance that stems from the success of just one person.

That's why you must be a success. Your success is contagious. You will inspire many, many people to greater levels of accomplishment and happiness in their lives and work simply by being successful yourself.

People who don't think they deserve success and happiness have merely forgotten that they do. You can tell them, "What do you think—God put us here to be miserable? Wouldn't that be a great creation? Come on! Creation is a megamiracle, and you and I are its greatest achievement so far. Of course we're here to be successful and happy!"

Perhaps the people who don't believe this have just been worn down by unwanted circumstances. Maybe nobody ever told them that they do, in fact, deserve to be happy. So tell them: *You deserve it!* It's a birthright and a responsibility as well as the greatest freedom you will ever experience. What's more, it's the perfect way to say thank you to the Creator who put this whole program together for us.

Your success is the gift you've come into this life to give. Of course, everybody has the right to *expect* success and happiness.

However, expectations alone, with nothing else to inspire them—such as a solid structure for accomplishment and a design of thought and action—remain just hollow expectations. Unless that condition changes, the chances are quite good that your expectations will never be fulfilled.

Expectations are powerful! Goals are powerful! The first step for making your goals and expectations real is to write them down.

Write Down Your Goals

In a famous study of the Harvard class of 1953, the researchers discovered that only 10 percent of the graduates had established goals at all and that only 3 percent had written down their goals.

Twenty years later, the researchers again interviewed the same class members, who were now involved in careers and families. They quickly determined that the 3 percent who two decades earlier had written down their goals were now worth more in economic terms than the entire remaining 97 percent of the class combined! Obviously, economic success isn't everything, but it certainly is a revealing and immediate way to measure the power of having written goals.

Until your goals are written down, they're not really goals; they are dreams and wishes. And if wishes were fishes, it would be the rare angler who would catch the really big ones.

Without a magic lamp, without action that's purposeful and by design, wishes rarely come true. We love fairy tales; most people do. They're the lottery of literature. But we will not bet our lives and the well-being of our families on a trail of bread crumbs scattered in the forest.

Writing your goals down in black and white forces you to focus on them. Then you will commit to them. Furthermore, it's important to share your goals with like-minded people—your champions.

Do you know what a champion is? In days of old, when knights were bold, an upper-class lady had a champion. He was a shining armor–clad character who defended her—life, honor, and all—against dastardly dragons, bad dukes, and any other negative assaults on her position or person. A champion is one who takes the field on behalf of another. Kings and queens all had champions, and you and I have them, too. Anyone who takes a stand for your greatness is your champion.

The way to live a life of accomplishment, fulfillment, and success is to have lots of champions, and the way to do that is to share your goals with committed, believing people and develop powerful partnerships with them. Be their champion. Championing others is a powerful way to catapult your own success.

The Three Legs of Accomplishment

Accomplishment is a three-legged affair, and it requires all three legs to stand solid and strong. You know how strong a tripod is: it can support hundreds of times its own weight—yet take away one leg, and it will instantly topple and fall. The three legs of accomplishment are the following:

1. Results
2. Growth
3. Fun

When you look at any of your accomplishments, you should be able to rate, on a scale of one to ten, what's true about them in each of these three areas.

A ten is perfect; nothing is missing. If you rate a given area less than a ten, then add to the score itself a statement about what's missing, which, when put in place, would make it a full-fledged ten. This will direct you toward any imaginative adjustments you need to make.

Too often people focus only on the results, but results gained without learning something or without having fun are incomplete. So is having fun without getting the result, or having fun without learning something new to help inspire you in the future. Accomplishment is all three.

A woman we knew in relationship marketing (we'll call her Charlotte) had the goal of earning ten thousand dollars a month. Charlotte's dream was to buy a beautiful house for herself and her family. She signed up with a dynamic company with great products and came out of the chute as though she had been shot from a cannon.

She worked long hours and ran all over the country building her business. Within four months, she was earning ten grand and then some. She hit twenty thousand dollars a month a few short months later. She could not have been more successful—or could she?

Actually, she realized that despite her financial success, she wasn't happy at all. She had her new house, and it was beautiful—it was all she had dreamed of, but she was never there to enjoy it. Her husband experienced such a shift in their relationship that he filed for divorce. Her kids had become strangers. Charlotte had achieved her financial goal and even surpassed it, yet she was miserable.

The point is that *results alone* are not enough. Be very clear about all you want to accomplish, and be sure in your goal-setting to include all those other things you want besides money, a new house, or a new car. Especially important are goals about your relationship with God, learning and development, relationships with family and friends, and having fun.

On your list of goals, make sure to notice where each goal has possibilities for fun, where the result is clear and concrete (which means measurable; we'll say more about that shortly), and where you will be learning new and better ways of being and doing—that is, where the goal provides for growth and development.

Remember, we are human *beings*, not human *doings*; goal-getting and accomplishment are more the result of who you are *being* than what you are *doing*.

Obviously, doing, or taking action, is vital. Nevertheless, remember that results themselves are the consequence of *who you are*; your actions are the natural outcome of your beliefs, values, purpose, attitudes, fears, desires, and habits of thought. Successful people, those who accomplish their goals, are being successful within themselves before they achieve the realities of success in the external, relative world of people, places, and things.

The point here is simply this: the most profound thing you can do to bring your goals to successful manifestation is to *be* a successful person. You can deserve and drive a Mercedes in your mind before you have one in your driveway. In fact, it's usually required. This doesn't happen overnight. Jeff Olson, in his great book, *The Slight Edge*, describes the accomplishment process as a few simple disciplines that in the act of doing don't seem to have any impact, but the compounding effect is powerful and brings the desired result. And he's right. We laugh a sad laugh when we hear that motivational gurus, pastors, and other leaders "inspire" their followers to a breakthrough. Are breakthroughs possible? Of course. But they are not the result of magic. They are the result of consistent, focused action and all of the principles we write and speak about all over the world.

Let's get back to the specifics of goal setting and goal getting. Setting and getting goals follow certain rules.

GOAL-SETTING SPECIFICS

Rule #1: Your goals must be concrete and have measurable results.

Wishy-washy goals aren't real goals. Airy-fairy goals aren't, either. Wishes and dreams and it-seemed-good-at-the-time ideas aren't goals at all.

Goals are solid and clear, and they can be measured and expressed in concrete terms. "I'm going to be a lawyer" is more of a dream than a goal. "I'm going to graduate from law school" or "I'm going to get my law degree" is quite different. Do you see how the second and third statements are more measurable, more concrete as a goal? "I'm going to get my law degree by June 30, 1995" is even more so.

It's really quite simple: if it can't be measured, it's not a goal.

"I'm going to be thin and trim." Really? How thin? How much will you weigh? How many inches will you be around the waist? Around the hips? Be specific with your goals. Clear and concrete goals have power. Foggy goals are for people who aren't willing to lay it on the line. If you have a vague, unspecified goal, nobody can say you failed when you don't reach it. Have courage. State powerful goals you can measure.

Rule #2: Set the goals you really want.

Don't make "process goals"; by this we mean don't make goals that are really only steps along the way to a goal. Of course, all goals always lead to new goals, but make your goals results that you actually want to achieve, not ingredients in the mix or part of the process. Go for the ultimate result you have in mind.

Having money, for example, is not a powerful or effective goal. Recall, from our discussion of values, this question: Why do you want the money? What do you want it for? Like digging down to the core of essential values, go to the core of a goal. That's the goal to write down.

Rule #3: Give your goals an ETA.

ETA means estimated time of arrival, what some people call a "by when." This is another instance in which specificity inspires. If there's no time frame, there's no reality. Until you assert your goal as an expected result by such-and-such a date, it's a wish, not a goal. (As a famous advertisement for a still-prosperous savings and loan company once said, "Wishing won't do it—saving will.")

Rule #4: State your goals as positive, present-tense accomplishments, complete with feelings.

Avoid expressing your goals as negatives or as desires sometime off in the future. Include an emotional payoff to supercharge your goal.

Let's take the example "I will quit smoking." Instead, you might state it this way: "I am living smoke-free—and I feel fantastic!"

Which of these two expressions stirs up some passion? Which of those two seems most likely to succeed?

Don't forget the time frame. "So by when will you be feeling great because you're smoke-free?"

"April 1, this year."

"Great!"

The more compelling your goals and the more passion they call forth from you, the more likely it is that you will hold them up and champion them—and that others will, too.

Working with Goals

Once you've established your goals, you'll need to work with them to bring them into being. One reason to write goals down is that this brings them closer to reality. Having an inspiration or imaginative idea, giving it focused thought, and then writing it down are all powerful steps in the success process. Do you see how each step is more concrete, more "real," than the one before?

Once your goals are written down, read them every day. If you want to, say them out loud as you read them. If you've designed your goals as we suggested—positive statements complete with feelings and a time frame—then your goals are powerful statements, and saying them aloud adds to their reality.

Have both short-term and long-term goals. Don't be afraid to use your imagination. Let your goals stand as real possibilities: not just a better version of the same old thing, but brand-new conditions and realities you've never accomplished before.

Remember, only when you aspire to excellence in your life can you be free from mediocrity. Because one of your goals must be constant growth and improvement, always ask yourself these questions: What can I do differently? What can I do better? What can I do best?

One key to knowing if your goal is on track is to check whether the goal makes you a little nervous. If your goal makes you sweat a bit, then the chances are that it's a really good goal—one that will stretch you and cause you to learn new and different skills as you go through the process of accomplishing it.

You've heard the term *movers and shakers*. Here's what that phrase means to us: people who are really moving are always shaking a little. Great goals, big goals, bring out the best in people.

It's been said that if you want to clear the fence when you're jumping over it and you aim for exactly that, you might make it and you might not. But if you shoot for the moon, no matter what, you're bound to clear the treetops. The bigger your goals, the better.

Remember the stretched rubber band? The bigger your goal, the more natural tension there is available to inspire you to bring it into existence.

Where the Getting Gets Good

Setting goals is one thing. Getting your goals is another. Effective goal-getting involves two simple steps:

1. Reverse goal-setting
2. Consistent focused action

Reverse goal-setting is simple. Look at your goal as a completed, present-tense accomplishment, and then ask yourself, "What had to happen just before that was achieved?" Write down your answer.

Now ask the question again about the specific accomplishment you just wrote down, and write *that* answer down. Then do it again, and keep doing it until you end up right where you are now, at your starting place. When you do this, what you'll have is a written plan that breaks down your goal into a series of doable steps. Through reverse goal-setting, even the most ambitious goal can be broken down into a series of smaller, progressive goals.

Once you have your goal laid out on paper in front of you in a sequence of subgoals, you can then design a strategy of actions to take. We recommend consistent focused action. Looking at your goal and at all the subgoals that have to be achieved to accomplish it, you'll be able to see what one thing you could focus on and do consistently that would bring you your goal.

TIPS FROM PETER

Several years ago, one of my goals was to publish my first book, *Living with Passion*, by the end of 1996.

I began the process of reverse goal-setting. What had to happen just before the book was published? It had to be printed. And before that? It had to be laid out as what printers call camera-ready. Before that it had to be designed and typeset, and the cover designed; before that it had to have a final edit, and before that a completed manuscript, and before that . . .

This process was a real eye-opener. When I started, I had no idea what it would take to publish a book, but after doing the reverse goal-setting, I had a really clear idea. Once I had the steps all laid out, I could see that in order to finish the book on schedule, I would have to write a chapter a week. My consistent focused action was to write one chapter a week. That required another consistent focused action, which was to write two hours each day, Monday through Friday. Then I discovered that I don't write very quickly. I spend a lot of time going back over things and thinking about better ways to say or illustrate something, so I quickly increased my two hours of writing to four hours per day. That worked fine.

I had my goal, and it had me moving—and shaking! I knew how important the book was going to be for people, so all my passion was called upon. I also had a step-by-step plan of action that would bring me my goal in the time frame I had planned. There were some things I didn't expect that backed me up a bit. But all in all, the book was completed, and it took a little less than twice as long as I expected. On the accomplishment scale, it was a twelve! (Remember, that's on a scale of one to ten.) I got the result, learned a tremendous amount, and had a ball.

Working with the independently owned, home-based business of relationship marketing also provides a perfect example of how goal-setting and goal-getting serve to clarify the path to accomplishment.

Unlike in a job working for someone else, in which your salary is pretty much set, in relationship marketing, the income you earn is up to you. This makes goal-setting a requirement for success.

When I first began my relationship marketing business, my goal was to earn a thirty-thousand-dollar monthly income. I set that figure down in the last box on a piece of paper that was divided into twelve one-month sections. The last square represented a time one year from the date I started.

I took that figure and calculated the total sales volume I needed to produce to earn thirty thousand dollars in commissions. It came to nearly six hundred thousand dollars. Well, that's a pretty big number, but I wasn't worried about it. I knew if I planned it out, working backwards from result to prior result, I'd end up having a clear picture of what I needed to do. I also knew that each individual step would be a whole lot smaller than that big ultimate dollar-volume goal.

When I finished all twelve months of my reverse goal-setting, I had a concrete plan for what was expected of me to reach my goal. I knew what dollar volumes I had to reach and when. I also knew how many distributors I would need in my organization to achieve those goals each month along the twelve-month plan. I also had the most important first step: make a prospect list. The step after that was also mapped out: call George—the strongest businessman on my list. He was on the very top of my list, so I started right in building my business.

I actually accomplished this goal in less time than I had originally planned. Again, there were surprises along the way (Murphy's Law is a universal constant!), but because I was prepared with a series of steps to take, nothing knocked me off-track. I handled all I needed to have done—and then some.

I knew clearly what it would take, and that removed the anxiety from my project. The whole process of having a goal, a one-at-a-time sequence of steps on the way, and a series of consistent focused actions all down in black and white took away any fears and replaced them with specific actions I knew I could take.

There may be a better way than reverse goal-setting and consistent focused action to get a step-by-step map of what to do, but we haven't discovered (or developed) it yet. It's powerful stuff.

Goal-setting is okay. Goal-getting is fantastic! We highly recommend it to everyone.

Rewards

When we're working toward a goal, one of the things we do to keep the whole process going and flowing is to give ourselves a reward every time we complete a subgoal. This is one element that's missing from most goal-setting and goal-getting systems—your rewards *along the way.* Some long-term goals take years to accomplish, so getting rewards for completing successful steps along the way is important for maintaining your passion and your focus.

Every time you develop a specific goal, make it part of the structure that you will grant yourself a reward upon successful completion of each subgoal as well as of the ultimate goal. Very important: make your reward something you would not normally do or give yourself. For instance, if you go out to dinner often, don't make that your reward. However, if you generally stay home for meals, the reward of going out to eat may be just right. New clothes, trips with the family—there are hundreds of special favors you can do for yourself that make the whole business of working on your goals more fun.

Appreciation and recognition are two of the most common human values, so reward yourself whenever you do a good job, no matter how easy or small the accomplishment.

Use this worksheet to establish your first goal and get started toward making it happen.

Goal

_____

_____

By when

_____

Reward

_____

Subgoal #1

_____

_____

By when

_____

Reward

_____

Subgoal #2

_____

_____

By when

_____

Reward

_____

Subgoal #3

_____

_____

By when

_____

Reward

_____

Subgoal #4

_____

_____

By when

_____

Reward

_____

Helpful Hints

Along with writing down your goals and doing the reverse goal-setting exercise, here are some other valuable elements to identify—in writing.

What obstacles will you need to overcome to complete your goal?

_____

_____

_____

What skills will you need to develop to complete your goal?

_____

_____

_____

Who are the people you'll need to speak with and the resources you'll need to have?

_____

_____

_____

What other knowledge will you need to reach your goals?

_____

_____

_____

If you need help identifying your goals, think about the next two questions.

1. *What things do I value most in my life?*
   Think about this question for as long and as hard as necessary to feel clear and secure with your answers. They

should determine where you want to go, who you want to be, what you want to do, and what you want to have.

2. *What have I always wanted to do but have been afraid to try?*

   This one provides valuable clues to parts of you that you may have buried away or filed under *N* for "no possibility." It puts you in touch with essentials: your values and your life purpose. Children are often asked a wonderfully simple question that gets to the heart of this: "What do you want to be when you grow up?" Sometimes that's a good question to ask ourselves!

Another great way to access these dreams and goals is to start the sentence "Someday, when I have the time, I'm going to . . ." and then fairly quickly, without giving it a lot of thought, complete the sentence in as many ways as you can. Then, on a fresh sheet of paper, do the same exercise, only starting out with "Someday, when I have the money, I'm going to . . ." You might be surprised—and pleased—at what comes out on the page.

Remember: people don't plan to fail; people fail to plan. Goals are planned actions you can take that in a very short time can change your life for the better and forever.

Your goals are the productive offspring of the marriage of your life purpose and your values. They are inspiration itself expressed on a local, individual, human scale. In short, goals— making them up, pursuing them, learning from the process, and bringing them into existence—give meaning to life. So this is especially important: don't sell out. To get a million dollars and give up your dignity is a bad deal!

To illustrate the concept of *meaning in life*, here's a favorite passage of ours from *Spoon River Anthology* by Edgar Lee Masters. In the book, Masters has all the people of a town speaking to the reader from their graves. Here's what one of the townspeople, George Gray, had to say:

> I have studied many times
> The marble which was chiseled for me—
> A boat with a furled sail at rest in a harbor.
> In truth it pictured not my destination
> But my life.
> For love was offered me and I shrank from its disillu-
>   sionment;
> Sorrow knocked at my door, but I was afraid;
> Ambition called to me, but I dreaded the chances.
> Yet all the while I hungered for meaning in my life.
> And now I know that we must lift the sail
> And catch the winds of destiny
> Wherever they drive the boat.
> To put meaning in one's life may end in madness,
> But life without meaning is the torture
> Of restlessness and vague desire—
> It is a boat longing for the sea and yet afraid.

You must not be afraid to unfurl your sails!

Set down your goals on paper. Read them. Take consistent focused action to accomplish them. When you do, you will catch the winds of destiny and live the rewards of joy and adventure that come to everyone sailing the stunning seas of life. Enjoy the ride!

"I don't understand. I talked to him on Sunday, and he seemed fine."

David Morgan sat on the bed in his dorm room, talking with his father on the phone.

"He was fine," his father, Patrick, said. "The doctor said it was a brain aneurysm that burst. He didn't even know he had it. He was dead by the time he hit the floor, so at least he didn't have to suffer a long illness. We can be grateful for that."

"OK. I just—you'll let me know when you get a flight scheduled for me? I can leave anytime, so just tell me when," David said.

"Sure, either your mother or I will call you back in a bit."

David sat on the bed for a long time after ending the call. Grandpa was dead. It was so hard to believe.

David and his grandfather, Dan Morgan, had been close from the beginning. David was the first grandchild; Dan had doted on him from the day he was born, and the boy had adored his grandfather just as much. Dan had taught him to fish, patiently helping him bait the hook and showing him how to remove the fish without getting finned. He'd attended David's baseball and basketball games, cheering louder than anyone else in the stands. When David became a teenager, Dan sometimes took him for weekend trips, and David had reveled in the individual attention now that his younger sister and brother were demanding more of his parents' time. When Patrick had driven David to college, Dan had come along for the five-hundred-mile trip—just the three guys. Now Dan was gone.

David remembered the last conversation he'd had with his grandfather. After the usual rundown of what each of them had done recently, Dan had said, "So your dad says you declared a business major. I'm glad you made a decision."

"Yeah, well, I pretty much had to do something. If I didn't declare a major this semester, I wouldn't be on track to graduate on time, so I had to pick something."

"Are you not happy with your decision?"

"I don't know. It's fine, I guess."

"What are you thinking you'll do after graduation? Go to grad school and get an MBA? Maybe go to law school? Do you have a field in mind?"

"No, I haven't really thought about it. I've got time."

"Yes, but not as much as you think. It's easy to let time slip by. You're going to need to get a grip on this pretty soon."

David hated these conversations. He'd had a few of them before when his parents had pressed him about declaring a major, and again with his academic adviser. He didn't understand what all the fuss was about. He made good grades. He had a B average without trying all that hard, and he even worked twenty hours a week. He was doing fine, and he'd figure out the future when it got here.

Dan had dropped the subject when he noticed that David was getting a little testy, but not before making one final comment: "All I'm saying is that if you don't take time to think about what you want out of life, it's awfully easy to wake up one day and find that you've just drifted along and you're someplace you don't want to be. That's what happens when you don't set goals."

David replayed the conversation in his head while flying home the next day. It made him feel uncomfortable, so he picked up the magazine from his lap and went back to reading it.

The next two days went by quickly. Family members arrived, there were long hours of greeting friends and acquaintances at the funeral home, and finally the funeral service took place on Friday. David felt at loose ends when all the activity died down, so he was happy to accept when Patrick asked him to help go through some of Dan's belongings on Saturday. He wasn't scheduled to fly back to school until the next day, and he had the feeling his dad would like the company as he sorted through so many memories.

They decided to tackle Dan's home office first. It was David's favorite room in the house. As a child, he'd often looked in amazement at the important-looking books that lined the walls. Once he asked his grandfather if he'd read all of them. "Yep, every one. Some of them twice," Dan had replied. It felt strange to be in that room without him.

"There sure were a lot of people at the funeral home," David said. "I didn't realize Grandpa knew so many people."

"Well, he lived here for more than forty years," Patrick responded. "He moved here right after law school and set up his practice. I guess he had thousands of clients over the years, and of course he knew most of the other attorneys in town, so a lot of them came to pay their respects. Then there were people from church, people he'd worked with at Habitat for Humanity and other places where he volunteered, people from his Kiwanis and Rotary Clubs. You're right, he knew a lot of people."

"That guy who did the eulogy was interesting. I liked the way he talked about all of Grandpa's accomplishments without making him sound like some kind of saint. I didn't realize Grandpa had done so much, or maybe I'd just forgotten a lot of things."

"He never slowed down, that's for sure."

David paused for a moment. "I guess he had a good life."

"I think so, and he seemed to think so. He always had a goal, and when he accomplished one, he'd move on to the next one. He said it kept him young," Patrick said. "Hey, why don't you go through the desk while I look through this file cabinet?"

David fell silent as he began sorting through the desk. It contained the usual items: pens, notepads, an address book, office supplies, and a financial ledger. When he got to the bottom drawer on the right, he pulled out a black leather-bound notebook that looked somewhat like the ledger he'd come across earlier.

"What do you want me to do with this, Dad?" he asked.

"What is it? More financial records?"

"I guess so," David said as he flipped it open. "No, actually it's something else."

The volume turned out to be a notebook filled with page after page of his grandfather's familiar handwriting. He turned to the first page. At the top, Dan had written "My Goals" with the date April 6, 1949, underneath. A list followed, numbered one through fifteen.

Next to the number one, Dan had written, "Graduate in the top 1 percent of my class."

Number two read "Go to Notre Dame Law School and graduate with honors."

The list went on.

"Read one book every week in addition to my school assignments."

"Learn to play the saxophone."

"Visit every continent."

David flipped through the book quickly. "Look at this, Dad."

"Oh, it's his book of goals. We need to keep this. It's a treasure."

"You know about this?"

"Sure, I used to see him writing in it sometimes when I was growing up. I'd forgotten about it though."

"The first page is dated 1949. How old was he then?"

"Let me think. He graduated from law school in 1958, so he must have finished college in 1955. I guess that would have put him in high school in 1949. A sophomore, maybe?"

"This is pretty amazing. He knew what he wanted to do way back then."

David moved to the large wingback chair in the corner and began to read the book more carefully. There was a new entry in 1951, coinciding with Dan's graduation from high school, and another two years later. The entries continued at intervals of three to five years, the last one dated the previous summer.

No items were crossed off any of the lists, but David noticed that there was a small, neat checkmark next to nearly all of them. That's how he had noted his accomplishments, David thought. Once an item received its checkmark, it was dropped from the next list while goals not yet attained were carried over.

David was fascinated. Each goal was stated in concrete terms. Many had self-imposed deadlines. "Read the complete works of Shakespeare by Dec. 31, 1964." "Complete five church mission trips before turning fifty." "Go skydiving on sixtieth birthday." Check, check, check.

Number twelve on the list dated 1972 was "Take an oil painting class." David looked up at the framed painting that hung over the desk. "I painted that myself," he remembered hearing his grandfather say with pride.

As he read through the list, David found himself remembering the eulogy he'd heard the day before. He'd been impressed with all that his grandfather had accomplished and all the people he'd touched. Now it was beginning to make sense. Offhand, David could match almost a dozen items on the various goals lists with accomplishments that had been mentioned during the eulogy. None of it had happened by accident. His grandfather had designed his own life by deciding what he wanted and making it happen.

"Is it okay if I keep this?" he asked.

"Sure," Patrick answered. "Let me make a photocopy of it, and then it's yours. I think he'd really like you to have it."

Back at school, David was immediately consumed with work. He had an accounting test to make up, and he was behind on his reading for nearly every class, so he threw himself into catching up. But he kept his grandfather's notebook on his desk, and every now and then, when he needed a break, he'd pick it up and thumb through it. "Take David to his first major league game." Check. "Take Gail to Italy for our thirty-fifth anniversary." Check. "Become president of the state bar association." Check.

One night around midnight, three weeks after his grandfather's death, David was about to turn out the light and get into bed when he had a thought. He rummaged through the small dormitory desk until he found a spiral-bound notebook from a class he'd taken last semester. Most of it was full, but there were several blank pages at the back. At the top of one page, he wrote "My Goals," followed by the date. This would be okay until he could get to the store and buy a proper journal.

It's a little sad to think that David had to lose someone so important to him before he learned the magic of setting concrete goals and working toward them. It would have been fun to see him share his first goals list with the man who inspired it and to see Dan's pride as he watched his grandson begin to check things off the list. But we like to think that in our somewhat childlike image of heaven, Dan had a big smile on his face when he saw David pull that spiral notebook out of the drawer and begin to write.

What about you? Have you started to bring your own goals into focus? We hope so, because we're ready to take the next step in living a significant life.

Adjust Your Attitude

Any fact facing us is not as important as
our attitude toward it, for that determines
our success or failure.
—*Norman Vincent Peale*

Attitude is the switch that turns on everything else. When you master your attitude, you master your life. If you're a good salesperson, you know that before a customer buys anything from you, he or she must first buy your attitude. The quality and effectiveness of all your communications, both personal and professional, is a matter of attitude. The attitude you have while you're with other people is the greatest influence on their thoughts and feelings. Your attitude means much more to people than what you say to them.

Have you ever heard it said that "People don't care how much you know until they know how much you care?" That's attitude—and that's power.

Have a conversation with somebody you know well. Choose a friend so as not to offend. While you're speaking to this person, keep telling yourself you don't care about him or her. Just keep saying in your head, "I don't care. I don't care. I don't care," and watch what happens. I'm certain you can imagine the outcome.

One of our goals is to have every person we speak with successfully cultivate an attitude of passion. We're convinced that an attitude of passion inspires peak performance. In fact, Peter's first book is all about cultivating passion, and his recorded voice-mail message even ends with the words "Have a great day—and live with passion."

Mastering Your Attitude

In the context of mastering your attitude, the word *mastering* means to rule and have authority over your attitude. We are convinced that the most powerful key to happiness and fulfillment is directing and managing your attitude. Every high-achieving leader is more than adept at this skill—and please understand that it *is* a skill and therefore it can be learned like any other skill. In fact, we could probably separate people into two broad categories: those who are masters of their attitude and those who are servants of their attitude.

How do you become a master of your attitude? How do you stay upbeat, especially during those tough times when the chips are down?

The answer is surprisingly simple. (Isn't that a joy!) Super-successful, fulfilled people continually run their own highlight films in the movie theaters of their minds.

You've seen short clips of spectacular athletic plays on the sports section of the evening news. That's what we mean. Successful, fulfilled people are always watching themselves make a diving catch, a spinning basket, or a world-breaking effort that results in a big, big win. They just change the game to fit their own circumstances.

When the going gets tough, the tough watch movies of themselves in positive, productive action. Another way of saying this is that successful people believe their own press.

We know, we know—we were taught not to do that. It's self-centered and ego-stroking, right? Not necessarily. Remember that your own success is the greatest gift you have to give to those whose lives you touch. You know the expression "When you laugh, the whole world laughs with you, but when you cry, you cry alone." Here's another way of seeing that: "When you succeed, the whole world succeeds with you, but when you simply try, you try alone!"

Your happiness is a gift. Cultivating a happiness habitude in yourself is in fact the very opposite of being egocentric. To be self-centered is to wallow in self-pity and mediocrity, to shrink from stepping up to the plate to swing the full home-run successes of which you're capable.

So go ahead—get your high-performance movies ready to play in your mind's screening room!

These highlight films of you in action can come from your own actual experience, or you can make them up. If you don't have some stock footage stored away in which you're doing the fantastic in a similar situation, use your imagination to make up a new one. Both are real in terms of how your mind perceives them.

This highlight film of yours will produce an immediate, positive result: a positive attitude. Seeing yourself at your best is the best way to shift your attitude into high (performance) gear.

You know that part of our vision is to instill passion in people. We intend and expect to persuade every one of you reading these words to demand more from life, to never again settle for less than the very best your life has to offer. After all, we reason, if we are made in God's image and likeness—and we absolutely believe we are—then how could we possibly accept mediocrity?

We can't. You shouldn't. And you won't!

If we approached writing this book with an attitude of "Don't worry, be happy," you'd probably respond to it with "Thanks a lot, but . . ." From reading this book so far, you know we feel much more passionately than that. You are—we all are—designed for happiness. So expect happiness! You deserve it. It's coming right at you, right now. That's the attitude we're writing with, and that's how we know this book is destined to encourage and inspire millions of people.

What's more, that's the attitude that we ask you to *read* these pages with.

Three Questions of Attitude

One of the most powerful ways of maintaining a positive attitude is to ask yourself powerful questions. These are the kinds of questions that will determine your focus and direct your actions. There are three questions we've found that are exceptionally powerful in generating and maintaining a positive, passionate attitude. Here they are:

Powerful Question #1: What's great about this?

No matter what the conditions around you, you can *always* find an answer to this question. It may be difficult at first. But really, all you need is practice.

TIPS FROM PETER

Once I had to be in San Francisco for a 7 a.m. breakfast presentation to two hundred representatives of Primerica Financial Services. The meeting was two and a half hours away from where I was staying at the time. So up and off I went, arriving at the same time the sun came up—and there were twelve people in the room.

Not two hundred. Twelve.

Okay, I said to myself, what's great about this? And my inner self began to grumble, "Well, up at four in the morning—pitch black, cold, damp—I drive two and a half hours. I expect two hundred people, and there are only twelve! Grumble, grumble . . . Hey! There is nothing great about this!"

But I knew from experience what this really meant. It meant that I had to ask the question again in a way that would get my attention. So I screamed it—inside my head, of course.

And then I realized that what was so great was the opportunity I had to inspire a dozen people to break through to new levels of passion, happiness, and success—which I would have slept through if I wasn't there.

I had my answer, but then an interesting thing happened—and it happens ninety-nine times out of a hundred when we ask ourselves this question. The "What's great about this?" answers kept coming.

Having only twelve people enabled me to be much more intimate with each person in the group. I could give each person individual attention, and we could all take more time on the points of my presentation, which would involve everyone more and make us more powerful as a group, because the quality of our relationships would raise the level of the work we were doing together two or three times what it would have been if the group were larger. We would be able to go deeper and higher, and the people would be able to interact more with me and among themselves, which always supercharges a group and results in bonding the individuals together as a team. I knew that when that happened, they would go back to their friends and families inspired and charged up, and that would cause a daisy-chain effect that would spread the word in a geometric way and eventually touch hundreds, even thousands of people, when all I did was meet with twelve. Wow!

You get the idea. The "What's great about this?" question almost always results in an attitude of gratitude as a fringe benefit. It simply comes free with the asking of the question. It's not even about having the "right" answer.

Powerful Question #2: What can I learn from this?

When we stop learning, our minds turn to mush. This is because the mind is the strongest muscle of all, and the old physical fitness slogan is true for mental muscle tone, too: use it or lose it! When Peter discovered that litigation law wasn't the key to happiness for him, and depression hit, he refused growth of any kind. He wouldn't pick up a book; he wouldn't engage in any meaningful conversation; he wouldn't even consider seeing what the Bible had to say to him. He simply stopped learning, and decay began to set in. Soon his thinking slowed, and everything else followed.

This can't be a halfway, maybe sort of thing. Learning must *never* stop. You can afford to skip a meal, but don't skip reading a book, because the information you don't get *can* hurt you!

A commitment at the level of complete devotion to lifelong learning is something we've discovered every high achiever shares. Asking this question often makes modeling the powerful success principle effortless and automatic.

Powerful Question #3: What has to change to make it happen?

There is always an *it*—the envisioned result—and a *change* that's required to bring *it* into being. It's another common characteristic of high achievers and people who lead happy, fulfilled lives. They're not only flexible; they have a love affair going with change. They have a *passion* for change—not just external change, but internal change. They understand that changing things within you comes before changing things around you, so they ride the waves of change like an expert surfer or like a dolphin.

People who are passionate about their living and working *love* change—and well they should, for it is the one and only absolute in this relative world of ours. Things will change; you can count on it.

"What has to change to make it happen?" is one constant question in the background for all people of passion. It keeps them open, upbeat, curious, innovative, and very productive.

One final point before we move on: all of the happy people we've studied believe that the best is yet to come.

The Servant Attitude

To inspire your success, you must develop an attitude about who you are that serves you: an attitude that strengthens your purpose, sets the stage for the full expression of your values, fuels your beliefs, and supports you in conquering your fears and accomplishing your goals and aspirations. For many people, the attitude that serves them best includes serving others.

TIPS FROM PETER

I was flying one day from Sacramento to Fort Lauderdale, Florida. The flight took off at 9 a.m. from California, and by 9:20 the man in the seat next to me was on his second Bloody Mary! It looked like it was going to be an interesting trip.

When the plane touched down in Florida, my seatmate was, to say the least, sloshed. I was in Good Samaritan mode, so I helped navigate him off the plane down to baggage claim, where we soon discovered that his bags were not to be found. I escorted this fellow over to lost baggage, where he promptly went ballistic, heaping loud, slurred verbal abuse on the airline attendant.

She was a saint. Calm and composed, she listened intently, nodding her head and apologizing to this angry, obnoxious, drunk passenger.

When my seatmate walked away to gain strength for another assault, I said to the attendant, "How do you deal with people like this all the time?"

She replied, "He's right. We shouldn't have lost his bags. And besides, see the sign?" she pointed above our heads. "It says Lost Bags. People don't come to me to thank us for their luggage arriving safely!"

The man returned and started in on her again. She calmly reached out her hand, put it on his arm, and said gently, yet with amazing strength, "Sir, currently there are two people in the world who care about your lost bags—and one of them is rapidly losing interest." She was incredible.

She finally located his bags, informed him they were on a flight that would arrive in an hour, took all his information down, and promised that his luggage would be delivered the moment it arrived. She would see to it personally.

I got my new friend into a cab, went back into the airport, and took a moment to tell that woman what a contribution she had made to me, what a statement she made about the power of attitude, and what a living example she was of servant leadership. I've never forgotten it or her.

———————————

You see, it's not the circumstances of our lives that determine our success; it's how we react and respond to those circumstances. And the *how* of that is our attitude. Author Stanley Judd said it perfectly: "You may be dead broke and that's a reality, but in spirit you may be brimming over with optimism, joy, and energy. The reality of life may result from many outside factors, none of which you can control. Your attitudes, however, reflect the ways in which you evaluate what is happening."

What kind of attitude do you need to cultivate to generate happiness and fulfillment? There are all kinds of powerful attitudes. An attitude of gratitude is one. An upbeat attitude is another.

There's a wonderful story about three bricklayers at a new building site. A visitor walks over to the first bricklayer and asks, "What are you doing?" The first worker looks up from his bricks and says, "What does it look like I'm doing? I'm laying bricks, you idiot!"

The man walks over to the second worker and asks again, "What are you doing?" The bricklayer looks over at him, slightly annoyed, and replies, "Can't you see, I'm building a wall?"

Finally, he approaches the third bricklayer and asks for the third time, "What are you doing?" The third bricklayer sits back, looks up at him, and says, "I'm building a hospital for sick kids so they can come here for help and get cured."

That's the kind of attitude you're looking for.

The Victim Dictum

As John Wooden, another legendary coach and master of successful living, put it, "Things turn out best for the people who make the best of how things turn out."

That's all positive thinking is: having a positive attitude.

TIPS FROM PETER

You can't let others determine your attitude. Before I realized this principle, I admit that I was one of the world's biggest victims. Even little things could incite me to anger or despair.

I remember driving down the parkway one day when a car from three lanes over on the left swerved across all the traffic and cut me off to exit. For hours after, I was railing and screaming about this incident and telling everybody who would listen (even people who wouldn't listen) about this jerk who had cut me off. Naturally, I got very little accomplished that day. Of course, that man, if he ever realized anything was wrong at all, probably forgot about me as soon as he exited the parkway. Why on earth should I have let that character affect my attitude for the whole day?

I have learned the strength and the power in three words: let it go. Now I realize that no one can harm me, bother me, or perturb me unless I accept the hurt. No one can inconvenience you unless you yourself say that you were inconvenienced. Eleanor Roosevelt said it this way: "No one can make you feel inferior without your consent."

All of the hurt, anger, disappointment, frustration, and other negative thoughts and feelings we blame on other people are completely not the truth. They all exist only in our own minds. We make them up. It's a matter of *our* attitude.

Motivational teacher and author Zig Ziglar tells a story about being in the Kansas City airport, tired, beat, and anxious to get home, when he learned his flight had been canceled.

"Fantastic!" Ziglar exclaimed.

The harried ticket agent looked as though Zig were the strangest thing she'd ever seen in her life, and she said, "Sir, I just told you your plane was canceled, and you replied 'Fantastic.' Why is that so fantastic?"

"Well," Ziglar said, "there must be a good reason to cancel the flight. It could be bad weather or a mechanical problem, and either way I think it's great that you and your people are looking out for my welfare and keeping me safe."

"I'm afraid the next flight I can get you on won't be for a number of hours," the agent said.

"Fantastic!" Ziglar replied.

Again, the incredulous agent asked, "And why is *that* fantastic?"

"Well, this is the first time I've ever been in this nice new airport. It's cold and wintry outside but warm and comfortable in here. There's a great-looking coffee shop over there, and I've got a lot of reading and writing to catch up on, so I'll just take advantage of the free office and get all my work done."

"Fantastic!" the ticket agent said with a smile.

"You bet!" Ziglar smiled back and went off to work in his free office with the convenient catering service.

Of course, Zig could have huffed and puffed, gotten all bent out of shape, and tried to bend everybody else, too, but the plane still wouldn't have left for hours. Either way, the *facts* of the trip would not have changed, but through his attitude the *experience* of the trip was totally transformed.

Positive attitudes lead to positive results. Remember, in both your personal life and your work life, before people buy anything you're offering, they buy your attitude—no matter what you're selling.

Reinventing the Past

We choose our thoughts, and our thoughts determine our attitudes. Once again, your thoughts and feelings influence the results you experience in your life much more than the other way around. As Anthony Robbins once said: "It is choice, not chance, that determines our destiny."

One of the most common attitude traps we all seem to fall into is keeping the past alive, and one important truth about the past is that it's always water under the bridge.

Wherever you are, be there! Are you old enough to remember the classic slogan of the 1960s, "Be here now"? Both of these statements are saying the same thing.

Being present in the present is the only way to relate to the world as it is. So much of the time we exist enclosed in a world composed of either our past opinions and judgments of people and circumstances or our fears about the future. Over time, these thoughts form the attitudes that become our habits of thought, or habitudes.

Our habitudes are such an important force in our lives because of the nature of the unconscious mind. The unconscious is an additive mechanism: it adds up all your experiences, thoughts, and feelings and decides which ones will be prevalent by keeping score. If you keep going over and over a negative experience in your conscious mind—as Peter did with that guy who cut him off on the parkway—each time you think it over, your mind takes it in as though it just happened again. That's what we mean by a habitude: a thought is repeated so much that it becomes an unconscious habit.

With such habitudes at work directing your imaginative energies, you can see how easy it is to stay in a rut you don't really want. To get out of these ruts, you have to break the hold the habitudes have on your mind, and you do that in exactly the same way you developed new beliefs and conquered old fears. Some experts call this *reprogramming*, and that's precisely what it is: a disciplined and focused effort to build a new, positive program—a positive habit.

We call it *reinventing the past*. You actually can re-create your own past by redefining events that have already occurred, giving them a new and more powerful meaning.

What would be different if Peter had defined the guy who cut him off as being a worried friend, husband, or parent rushing to the hospital, instead of an inconsiderate jerk out causing danger with his carelessness?

In his superb book, *The 7 Habits of Highly Effective People*, Stephen Covey, speaking about paradigm shifts, tells one of the most powerfully moving stories you will ever hear or read.

Covey was sitting on a New York subway one Sunday morning when a man entered with his two kids. The children were as wild as could be, tearing up and down the subway car, grabbing people's newspapers, and disturbing everybody. They were behaving like brats, and all the while, their father just sat there staring at the floor, seemingly oblivious to his children's rude and destructive behavior.

Finally, Covey could take it no longer, so he remarked to the man that his kids were a mess and he ought to be more responsible.

The guy looked up at him with vacant, sad eyes and apologized. Then he told Covey that they had just come from the hospital where his wife—the kids' mother—just died. He said he supposed that the children didn't know how to deal with that, so they were going a bit nuts, because they didn't know what else to do. Again, he said, he was sorry.

Wham!

In an instant, Covey completely changed his mind—shifted his opinion and judgment of what was happening right in front of him—180 degrees.

It is sad that we often need such dramatic and even heartbreaking information to shift how we're thinking about things. There is powerful truth in the Native American wisdom "Walk a mile in the other man's moccasins before you pass judgment on him."

This is all part of developing a high-achieving, happiness-producing attitude. Live each day as though it were your last, with passion and with excellence. Yesterday is over, and tomorrow may never happen. Today is all we have.

This is not a limiting belief; on the contrary, it is tremendously powerful. It brings an end to procrastination, and it marshals a passion and desire to achieve all the good things that we know we can achieve, because when we live each day as though it were our last, we live each day to its greatest potential.

As Crazy Horse, along with other Lakota warriors, said at the Battle of the Little Bighorn, "It is a good day to die."

"When Do I Die?"

A doctor once had a patient, a thirteen-year-old girl, who needed blood to live. The doctor walked over to the girl's younger brother, who was sitting in the visitors' room, and asked, "Davy, I need your blood to save your sister; will you help us?"

The little boy gulped but said yes without hesitation. Davy would do anything to help save his sister's life.

The doctor laid Davy down on a table and started removing blood from one of his veins to transfuse directly into his sister. The family and the doctor prayed as they watched the girl in silence. Miraculously, in half an hour she was over the crisis. She would live. They were all elated, including Davy.

Then, through teary eyes, Davy asked, "Doctor, when do I die?" Davy thought that he was giving *all* of his blood to his sister. He thought that he had agreed to die for his sister.

There's a great spark that is in all of us. The story of young Davy's courage can help us find such a spark in ourselves.

I'm not suggesting that you have to die, or even be willing to die, in order to be a success. These stories are powerful illustrations of beliefs and attitudes that simply cannot be broken. They show us what it can be like to have the kind of passionate, courageous attitude that inspires any effort, any enterprise, and any life purpose—no matter how grand.

Living with a thirteen-year-old girl is rarely easy, and Megan Murphy was no exception. She could go from laughing to crying in the blink of an eye, usually leaving her parents bewildered about what had prompted such a sudden change. "She's weird" was the usual response from her younger brother, Ben.

Her parents, Mark and Amy, had braced themselves for their children's teenage years, but the reality had still come as a shock. Their oldest child, Brian, had become reclusive, lethargic, and argumentative, but this behavior had gradually disappeared by the time he finished high school and left for college.

Almost before Mark and Amy could exhale and congratulate themselves on having successfully navigated raising a teenager, Megan turned thirteen and seemed to change overnight. The formerly sweet child who had loved to snuggle with her parents on the sofa now barely spoke to them. The little girl who had loved family outings morphed into someone who was embarrassed to be seen in public with them, even ducking below the car windows if she spotted her friends.

Although her relationship with Mark remained fairly stable, Megan and Amy seemed to be constantly engaged in a battle of wills. A typical conversation went something like this:

Amy: Megan, please take your dirty dishes into the kitchen and put them in the dishwasher.

Megan: In a minute. I'm busy right now.

Amy: You're texting with someone. That can wait, and this will only take a minute.

Megan: I'll do it later. Besides, they're not hurting anything.

Amy: That's not the point. They belong in the kitchen.

Megan: Then you take them. You're the one who cares.

Amy: Don't talk to me like that. I asked you to do something, so do it.

Megan: In a minute. I'm busy right now.

Amy: Who are you texting?

Megan: Nobody.

Amy: Clearly you're texting someone. All I'm asking is—oh, for heaven's sake. I'm going to take a bath. Take your dishes into the kitchen.

More often than not, the evening would end with Amy returning to the family room to find that Megan had gone to bed and the dirty dishes were still on the coffee table.

"I swear, I don't know what we're going to do with her," Amy said one evening as she and Mark took a walk through their neighborhood. "I feel like all I do is nag her about everything. Chores, homework, picking up after herself. Everything is an argument with that girl."

Mark always tried to be sympathetic and supportive during these conversations, but it was a little hard for him to relate. He still had a pretty good relationship with his daughter. She didn't actively engage him the way she did Amy. He'd had some problems with Brian when he was in high school, but usually they'd still been able to connect through their mutual interest in sports. Maybe they hadn't talked for hours about deeply personal issues, but they'd certainly been able to discuss whether the Cubs would ever win a pennant and how the Lakers had managed to blow a twenty-two-point lead in last night's game. It wasn't the same with Megan, but they usually got along fine. She seemed to save most of her animosity for her mother.

"I could never have gotten away with talking to my mother like that when I was her age," Amy went on. "I had more chores than she does, and I always got them done. I did my homework, kept my grades up, had good friends, and treated my parents with respect. I just don't get this."

"I know," Mark said. "We got through it with Brian, and I guess we'll get through it this time." He knew his response wasn't particularly helpful, but he didn't have another answer.

The next weekend, Amy was busy, so Mark volunteered to drive Megan to the mall to meet some friends. He decided to take advantage of the occasion to talk with Megan about her issues with her mother. The moment he broached the subject, he found himself on the receiving end of his daughter's typical eye roll and heavy sigh.

"She drives me crazy," she said. "She's always lecturing me about how responsible she was when she was my age. I'm sick of it. She's forever butting into my business, wanting to know who I'm talking to and what time I'll be home and who's going to be at the party. Why should she care about that stuff? I'm entitled to privacy."

"I'm sure she doesn't mean to—" Mark began, but Megan cut him off as though she hadn't heard him.

"Like today. I had to play twenty questions with her before she'd let me go to the mall. What does she think I'm going to do, anyway? Smoke pot in the food court? God, she makes me so mad. And I'll get another interrogation when I get home. Who did you see? Where did you go? Did you buy anything? I hate her."

"Okay, that's not acceptable," Mark said quickly.

"I know, I know. I guess I don't really hate her, but she's making my life miserable."

"Well, honey, you're not exactly making her life a picnic, either," Mark said as he pulled up to the mall entrance. "I'll pick you up at eight sharp."

A few weeks passed, and the battle of wills between the Murphy women continued to escalate. When Amy's sister asked if her daughter, Carol, could spend the weekend while she and her husband attended an out-of-town wedding, Amy readily agreed. Maybe having someone else in the house would provide a buffer for a couple of days.

Megan was excited. Carol had just turned seventeen, and Megan idolized her. She could drive and date, and her life seemed to be just about perfect, as far as Megan was concerned.

On Friday night, Carol and Megan were sitting on the back porch chatting when Amy came outside. "Oh man, what does *she* want?" Megan muttered.

"I thought you girls might like some cookies," Amy said. "They're still warm from the oven."

"Thanks, Aunt Amy," Carol said. "They smell great."

When Amy had returned to the house, Megan said, "Sorry about that."

"What's the matter? Your mom is cool," Carol responded.

"Are you kidding me? She's the least cool person in the world. Trust me."

"What's wrong with her? She seems fine to me."

"Okay, let me give you an example," said Megan. "Last weekend my friend Carly was having a party. Everybody was going. First, my mom wouldn't let me go until she called Carly's mother to be sure some adults would be there. Can you believe that? She called her mother! I was so embarrassed. Then she asked me about a million questions about who'd be there and what we'd be doing and what time I'd be home. She even wanted to know what I was going to wear. And the worst part? When I got home, she checked my breath to see if I'd been drinking. She said that wasn't what she was doing, but I could tell by the way she hugged me and got real close to my face. She doesn't trust me at all."

"Maybe she thinks you're being secretive because you don't volunteer any information," Carol suggested.

"Why should I? I can take care of myself. That stuff is none of her business. I can't wait until I'm your age and have my own car and can do exactly what I want."

"Well, that's not quite how it works!" Carol said with a laugh. "I still have a curfew and rules, but things have lightened up between me and my mom. We used to butt heads all the time, but then about a year ago something happened that made both of us change our attitudes."

"What happened?"

"We were like you and your mom. I felt like she didn't trust me, and she felt like I was lying and hiding stuff from her. The more she questioned me, the more secretive I got. It just went around and around."

"Yeah, that's how we are. It's crazy."

"So one weekend I went to a party at this guy's house. I didn't really know him that well, but he seemed cool. His parents were out of town, so a bunch of people brought booze, and it started to get pretty wild. I drank a little bit, but I wasn't wasted or anything. I was dancing and having a good time when one of my friends came over and said something was wrong with Heather and that I should come and help. Heather was on the floor of the bathroom, passed out cold. Turned out she'd been drinking tequila shots all night. I leaned down and tried to wake her up, but it didn't even seem like she was breathing very much.

"I wanted to call an ambulance, but the guy who was having the party said no, because he'd get in trouble. He said she'd just sleep it off in a couple of hours. I said I'd take her to the hospital myself if someone would help me get to into my car, but he grabbed my purse and wouldn't let me leave. By that time, other people were getting scared, too, and the place cleared out really fast. Heather was looking worse and worse, and I really thought she was dying. We'd gotten all those lectures about alcohol poisoning at school, but I guess I didn't think it really happened."

"Wow, what did you do?"

"Finally I said I was going to get a pillow to put under Heather's head, and I started looking for my purse. I couldn't find it, but I did see a phone in the guy's parents' bedroom, so I locked myself in there and called my mom. I knew I'd be in trouble, but I didn't know what else to do. She was really good about it. She told me to stay in the bedroom and she'd call an ambulance. Mom got there right behind the police and the ambulance. Heather was in the hospital for like three days. The doctor told her parents she'd probably have died or had brain damage if she hadn't gotten there when she did."

"So how much trouble were you in?"

"It was weird. My mom didn't really talk about it that night. She just said she was glad I was okay and that I'd done the right thing by calling her. She said she was disappointed that I'd gotten myself into that situation because I knew it was against the rules, but she was proud of me for handling it well. She said that she hoped I understood now how easy it was for a situation to get out of control and why she was always so concerned about where I was going and who I'd be with.

"Then she said, 'How about we both agree to change our attitudes a little bit? I'll try to trust you more, and you try to be a little more forthcoming with me.' I was so grateful that I wasn't grounded that I decided to play along for a few days, but I was shocked at how much easier our relationship got. After that, we just fell into the habit of being more open and trusting each other more, and things just kept improving."

The story stayed on Megan's mind for the next few days. She knew she was basically a good kid. She didn't smoke or drink or do drugs. She and her friends all got good grades. In fact, she really didn't have anything to hide from her parents. She just liked her privacy, but maybe her secrecy was sending a different message. She decided to try an experiment.

The next day, she casually approached Amy as she was cutting vegetables for a salad. "Is it okay if I spend the night at

Carly's Friday?" she began. Before Amy could respond, Megan continued, "Amanda is going to be there, too. Carly's mom said she'd take us to the skating rink, then we're going to rent a movie and make our own pizza. You need to pick me up at 11 Saturday morning because Carly has a dentist appointment at 11:30. You can check with her mom if you have any questions."

Amy stopped chopping and thought for a moment. "No, I guess I don't have any questions. That sounds fine."

During the ride home from Carly's house on Saturday morning, Amy said, "Did you have a good time?"

Megan started to bristle. This was none of her mother's business. Why was she always so nosy? She started to roll her eyes and make a biting remark, but stopped to reconsider. "I did," she said. She briefly described the pizza they'd made and the movie they'd watched, then braced herself for her mother's follow-up interrogation.

"That sounds great," Amy responded. "We should make our own pizza at home sometime."

Over the next few weeks, Megan continued her experiment. She found that the less combative she was, the less her mother nagged. The more information she provided willingly, the less Amy pressed for more.

"I can't get over the change in her," Amy told Mark as they got ready for bed one night. "It's not perfect, but that belligerent attitude has almost disappeared. I think it might be okay to let her go on vacation with Carly's family after all. I was going to say no because I didn't know what she might get into, but now I'm leaning in favor of it."

"I'm glad you two are getting along better," Mark said. "Things are a lot more pleasant around here."

The next day, Amy agreed to drive her daughter to the mall. Megan looked thoughtfully out the window as they drove in companionable silence. Finally, as they were approaching the mall entrance, she spoke up.

"Mom, can I tell you something?"

"Sure, honey."

"I like being around you a lot more since your attitude has improved."

Amy was stunned. *Her* attitude? She glanced over at her daughter, but the sarcastic look she'd been expecting wasn't there. Apparently she was serious, so why argue?

"Thanks, Megan," she said. "I'm glad you noticed. That means a lot to me."

Amy wasn't nearly ready to be a grandmother, but a small part of her suddenly realized that she couldn't wait to watch Megan raise a teenage daughter.

If you've ever been the parent of a smart-mouthed kid, you might have uttered the words, "Don't give me that attitude!" at least once or twice. Our attitude helps to shape not only how others see us but also how we see ourselves and even, to a great extent, how happy we are. Megan's eye-rolling and "nobody suffers like I do" demeanor weren't making her any happier. It made her life harder, not easier. Once she started to realize that the attitude she presented to others—good or bad—helped to determine how she was treated, things began to look up for her and for those around her.

What will it take for you to do that? Keep reading.

Embrace Challenge

Accept the challenges so that you may
feel the exhilaration of victory.
—*General George S. Patton*

Challenge is a major catalyst for success. Happiness is a challenge. We challenge you to become all that you can be—and more. Even more than that, we challenge you to have a blast doing it! We make such an outlandish challenge because we want you to understand that meeting a challenge head-on is a joy.

Can you imagine that? Some people cannot. Some people hold challenge as an undesirable nuisance, or worse, a thing to be avoided at any and all costs. It's too much work, and that's a shame, because not only can a challenge be truly powerful, it also holds a hidden secret. Once you know this secret, it makes all the challenges you face in your life and work a joy to deal with.

Ready? Here it is: A challenge is not the truth. *Challenge* literally means "false accusation." Trace the word back through the Middle English *calenge* and Old French *chalenge*, all the way to the Latin *calumniari*—they all turn out to mean "accuse falsely."

This means that a challenge is simply not the truth; it's something that's made up. All of us make up challenges to serve our needs, our desires, and our purposes. Thus, a challenge is something that is *not yet* true. It is not a lie; it's a dream, a hope, or an obstacle to overcome, but one that has not yet been achieved. That puts a new light on challenge, doesn't it?

So when we use the word *challenge* in this book, we're clear that we're making it up to serve our mission, which is to have millions and millions of people living a significant life.

The greatest challenges you can develop are those that inspire you. Don't bother with challenges that serve only to distract or frustrate you. Remember that challenges are not the truth, so you get to choose whether to entertain them.

Discard any challenges in your life that don't inspire and encourage you, that do not serve your success and ability to choose a life of significance.

We used to avoid challenges—or attempt to—but not anymore. In our lives today, both of us actively seek challenges, ferret them out, and make them up whenever we can, because we've caught on to their power to give us power. We consider ourselves connoisseurs of fine challenges—we're challenge nuts, in fact. "Our names are Peter and Robert. We are challenge-aholics." And we recommend that you be the same.

Probably no other football coach in history was as successful as the legendary Vince Lombardi of the Green Bay Packers, who coached throughout a successful career, then retired, and then came back to coach again. One of his legions of admirers, Tommy Prothro, said that he, too, would "like to win every game, but I'm not sure winning would mean much if I always won. I think that's why Vince quit. He'd won too much. He came back because he missed it, but by then he had a new challenge—making a comeback."

One of the greatest perceived challenges given in biblical times was the one God gave to the ancient Hebrews before they entered the land of Israel. God gave them the land and told them to take possession of it. The challenge was really a figment of the people's imaginations, however. The Hebrews had two choices. They could accept God at His word and confidently take the land. That would have been a good choice. Unfortunately, they made the other choice. Rather than believe God, they believed a few spies who said that the land would be impossible to conquer. They *made up* a negative challenge that was absolutely not the truth, and that cost them years of trouble.

Then there was King David, who made up challenges to inspire himself. Before he was crowned king, a giant of a man named Goliath, a Philistine who was more than nine feet tall, challenged the people of Israel: "Choose a man and have him come down to me. If he is able to fight and kill me, we will become your subjects, but if I overcome him and kill him, you will become our subjects and serve us" (1 Samuel 17:8–9). Nobody wanted to be a slave of the Philistines. The people were understandably a bit nervous.

But not David. David was strengthened by these words. He said to the giant, "You come against me with sword and spear and javelin, but I come against you in the name of the Lord

Almighty, the God of the armies of Israel, whom you have defiled. This day the Lord will hand you over to me, and I'll strike you down and cut off your head." David "ran quickly toward the battle line to meet him" (1 Samuel 17:45–46, 48). God did what David had said, and so did David.

David knew that Goliath's challenge was not really a challenge at all but something the Israelites had made up because they lacked the faith David possessed. David knew that running away from battles was the one sure way to keep them coming after us. How many of us are making up our own Goliaths? Accepting a positive challenge has a powerful and lifelong impact not only on those of us who accept the challenge but also on many others around us.

A routine of constant challenge builds strong beings in much the same way that a good gym workout builds strong bodies. Challenge makes you strong by exercising your creative mental and emotional muscles. Challenge tones your intuition and imagination, exercises your desire, puts mass on your positive beliefs, trims the fat off your fears, and adds definition and articulation to your attitudes. Challenges are the free weights you use to train for success and fulfillment.

Chris Denning sat in his regular booth in the Eastside Diner, sipping his third cup of coffee and reading the morning newspaper. Since retiring four months ago, he'd gotten into the habit of having breakfast there a few mornings each week. It was a good excuse to get out of the house, and often he would run into a friend or two from the neighborhood, guys who had also retired and had plenty of time on their hands.

This wasn't how Chris had envisioned his so-called golden years, an expression that never failed to annoy him. He and his wife, Lynn, had planned to buy a recreational vehicle and travel around the country, sometimes taking along a grandchild or two during the summer, but those plans evaporated when Lynn had suddenly died of a heart attack. Chris had continued to work for almost two years, but his passion for practicing law seemed to have died along with Lynn, and he decided to leave it to the younger attorneys. After all, he'd had a career of more than forty years, and he'd built one of the area's most prestigious law firms from the ground up. It was time to call it quits and take it easy.

Overall, he liked being retired. He got a bit lonely sometimes, but he enjoyed having time to read, fish, and volunteer at his church. His son, Kyle, and his family lived nearby. Chris had dinner with them every couple of weeks, and he had become a regular fixture in the bleachers at his grandchildren's ball games. He'd invested well, so money wasn't an issue.

He was folding his newspaper and getting ready to leave when Donna, one of the waitresses, approached his table. "Can I get you another cup of coffee, Mr. Denning?" she asked.

"No thanks, I think I've had my limit for today," he replied. "I'm going to head home and do a little work in the garden."

"Okay, then, have a good day." Donna started to leave, then turned back and asked hesitantly, "Can I ask you something?"

"Sure, what's up?"

"You're a lawyer, right?"

"Well, I used to be. I'm retired now. Do you have a legal problem?"

"Not me. Jorge, a guy who works back in the kitchen."

"Okay, why don't you sit down and tell me about it?"

Donna sat down across from Chris and began. "His life is just falling apart. He used to work at that tire factory on

Route 12, but of course he lost his job when it closed down a few months ago. The only job he's been able to find is here, but they can only use him a few hours a week, and he makes next to nothing. Now he's been evicted from his apartment, which really stinks. I mean, I get that you have to pay rent, but it doesn't seem fair to just put someone out on the street, especially when they have a child."

"Oh, he has a family?" Chris asked.

"Just a six-year-old son. He's a single dad. I'm not sure what the situation is with Joshua's mother, but I know she doesn't live around here. She might have even moved back to Guatemala. That's where they're from."

"Is Jorge here legally?" Chris asked carefully.

"Oh yeah, but he doesn't know for how long. He's afraid that without a job or a home, he'll lose his son and maybe even be deported. Apparently something similar happened to a guy he knows, and now he's terrified."

"Where is he living now?"

Donna hesitated, then leaned forward and whispered, "In his car. With a child. Can you imagine?"

"Wow, that's really rough," Chris said.

"Anyway, I was wondering if you could talk to him. I know it's a lot to ask, and of course he wouldn't be able to pay you, but I think he needs to know what his legal options are, and you're the only lawyer I know." When Chris didn't respond immediately, she added, "He speaks good English," as though she hoped that would seal the deal.

"I'd be happy to talk to him, Donna, but I don't know how much I can help. I was a corporate attorney. I've never dealt with immigration law, but I'd be happy to talk with him. Can he meet me here at the coffee shop? Tomorrow morning, maybe?"

"That would be great. I don't think he's working tomorrow, so he should be free to stop by after he drops Josh off at school at 8:30. You're usually here around that time, anyway. Thank you so much, Mr. Denning. Jorge is such a nice guy, and he really doesn't deserve this."

"Not a problem. I'll see you and Jorge tomorrow," Chris said. As he headed home, he told himself that he really needed to be more grateful for his own good fortune.

The next morning, just as Chris was polishing off the last of his scrambled eggs, Donna appeared at his booth with a shy-looking young man. Jorge, who appeared to be in his late twenties, shook Chris's hand and sat down.

"Donna tells me you're having a rough time. I'm sorry to hear that," Chris began.

"Yes sir, things have gone badly for me since I lost my job, and they just keep getting worse," Jorge said.

"I explained to Donna that although I'm an attorney, your situation isn't within my area of specialty," Chris warned. "Why don't you tell me everything that's going on, and maybe I can help you figure out where to go from here, but I'm thinking we may need to find someone with more experience in immigration law."

"I understand," Jorge said. "I appreciate you taking time to talk to me."

Chris listened carefully as Jorge began to recount his litany of problems. He had been in the United States on a work visa for nearly ten years, but his visa was due for renewal soon, and he was concerned that it wouldn't be extended if he didn't have a job. His only income was from the diner, but the owner only needed him for a few hours a week, so Jorge barely made enough money to feed himself and his son. There was nothing at all left over for housing. They'd been sleeping in Jorge's car for the past few nights, but clearly that was not a permanent solution.

"Have you tried one of the shelters?" Chris asked. "Obviously that's not ideal, but it would be better than living in your car."

Jorge leaned forward and spoke emphatically. "Yes! I went there right away, but they said we didn't qualify."

"How could you not qualify? You're homeless."

"The woman told me that the shelters are too crowded, so they can't take everyone who comes in. If you have family, they think you can stay with them, so they say you don't qualify."

"You have family in the area?"

"No! That's the problem. I have family back in Guatemala. The woman at the shelter said that as long as Joshua and I have family there, we have a place to live and can't stay at the shelter."

"But you've lived here for nearly ten years, and if your son was born here, he's a U.S. citizen."

"I know, that's what I said, but she said that's their policy."

As they continued to talk, more issues arose. Jorge was afraid that Joshua would be taken away from him if anyone found out they were homeless. He was afraid Josh wouldn't be able to attend his school anymore if it was discovered that they no longer lived in the right district. Jorge was afraid he'd be arrested for vagrancy if the police discovered him sleeping in his car. He was afraid he'd be deported, and then what would happen to his son? He was, very simply, afraid.

Before leaving the restaurant, Chris gave Jorge his phone number and told him to contact him if anything came up. "Give me a couple of days to make some calls and get up to speed on situations like this," he said. "I'll leave a message for you here as soon as I have some information."

Driving home, Chris turned the situation over in his mind. He knew the attorneys at Legal Aid were already overworked, so he thought he'd find an immigration lawyer who would agree to take Jorge's case without charging a fee, as a favor to Chris, and let that attorney take it from there.

But in the back of his mind, Chris had begun to realize that Jorge's situation wasn't just an immigration problem. His legal status was just one component of a much larger issue. There were thousands of people in Jorge's situation: unemployed or underemployed, homeless, many with children, and nowhere to turn. Many of them, perhaps most of them, were U.S. citizens. With the exception of the immigration issues, they faced the same hurdles Jorge was experiencing. How many other Jorges were out there? And who was helping them, or were they simply falling through the cracks?

By the time he fell into bed that night, Chris was mentally exhausted. He'd quickly located an attorney who had agreed to help Jorge work out his visa situation, but Chris was unable to stop thinking about the myriad of other issues Jorge had mentioned. Rather than driving to a nearby stream for a little trout fishing, he'd found himself spending the day scouring the Internet, boning up on the legal hurdles faced by the homeless. There seemed to be no shortage of them.

During the next few weeks, Chris continued to forgo his usual pursuits in favor of learning more about the city's homeless population. He met with Legal Aid lawyers, the directors of shelters and soup kitchens, government officials, and church leaders who had programs to address those issues. He talked with dozens of people who lived at the shelters and ate at the soup kitchens, taking careful notes about the problems they faced each day, many of which he'd never even considered.

He learned that when people lost their homes, their possessions fell away, disappeared, or got lost, sometimes including important documents like their birth certificates and Social Security cards. Without those, it was difficult to get a job, but often people didn't know how to go about replacing them. As a result of the economic downturns, many people were shocked to find themselves homeless for the first time, and they knew nothing about applying for government benefit programs. They had never thought they'd need those things. Child support and custody issues, criminal charges, eviction, employment problems—the list seemed endless.

Chris had always been a man who liked a challenge. Law school had been challenging, but he'd graduated near the top of his class and moved on to tackle the challenges of starting his practice and becoming good at his job. Then he began to expand his firm, bringing in new associates and working to build its reputation. He had become active in his local and state bar associations, eventually serving as president of each. Along the way he had eagerly taken on the challenges of becoming a husband and a father. Things leveled out a bit in the last few years of his practice, but he had never failed to enjoy the challenge of a new case.

Retirement had been different. He liked many things about his leisure pursuits, but he began to realize that he missed the mental stimulation he'd always gotten from work. Now his biggest challenges consisted of what to make for dinner and what to do about an investment when it stopped performing well.

Since his initial meeting with Jorge, Chris had felt challenged again, and it felt good. This was an entire field of law he'd never even considered, and he was fascinated with it. From the minute he woke up in the morning, his mind was racing with new ideas and possibilities. There were a lot of people out there who needed help. Maybe he was the guy who could provide it.

Six months later, Donna approached Chris's booth in the diner, coffee pot in hand. "Another cup, Mr. Denning?"

"No thanks, I've got to get moving. Busy day."

"I can't believe you went back to work. Who's going to catch all the fish now?"

"Oh, I still have time for that, but somebody's got to mind the store. I've got two other retired lawyers working with me now, plus a paralegal and a few law students who help out. We're already doing regular free clinics at two shelters, and tomorrow I'm meeting with the director of the soup kitchen on Shelby Street to talk about setting up shop there for a few hours a week. There's plenty to do."

"I never thought asking you to talk to Jorge would lead to all that, but look at you, saving the world," Donna said.

Chris laughed as he stepped out of the booth and picked up his briefcase. "I'm working on it."

It would have been easy for Chris to help Jorge fix his problem and return to the comfort of his retirement. Instead, he eagerly turned a casual encounter into a challenge that gave his mental muscles a workout and instantly brought a new level of significance to his life.

Are you ready to follow Chris's example? If so, take a moment to think about a challenge you're currently facing or, better yet, one you'd like to create for yourself. Once you've named that challenge, you're ready to move ahead to the next step on the way to significance.

Pinpoint Your Priorities

It's not enough to be busy; so are the ants. The
question is, what are we busy about?
—*Henry David Thoreau*

E ach year, you're granted 525,600 minutes, which the
universe doles out in increments of 1,440 per day. Aside
from doing the necessities like sleeping and eating, how
are you spending these minutes? A better question might be this:
Are you merely "spending" them, or are you *using* them to reach
your goals and achieve a life of significance?

We've done a lot of work up to this point. We've fueled your
desire, found your purpose, fired up your imagination, sharpened
your focus, set some worthwhile goals, gotten an attitude check,
and learned to embrace challenge. But let's be honest with ourselves. None of those things will make much difference if you

fail to take one absolutely essential step, and that's establishing priorities and using them to guide how you use your time. Without that step, a year from now you'll still have your purpose, your goals, and your go-get-'em attitude, but you'll probably be no closer to bringing real significance into your life.

Earlier, we touched on the topic of setting priorities when we talked about reverse goal-setting and consistent focused action. Using those techniques should help you to determine what specific steps you need to take to reach the goals you've set for yourself. Now the challenge is to make sure those steps become true priorities in your life and therefore find a place on your daily to-do list.

You might want to begin by taking a hard look at how you're spending your time now. For a few days, keep a record and make it as specific as possible. It might be a real eye-opener to realize just how much time you spend checking and rechecking your e-mail, chatting with coworkers, or putting out office brushfires, none of which are leading you toward a more significant life.

But even beyond those little time-wasters, how many of your current activities have little or nothing to do with the goals you've established? This isn't a book on time management (although we encourage you to explore that topic for help in freeing more of your time for the things that really matter to you), but we've found it useful to ask ourselves a few simple questions to determine the value of activities that tend to suck up time like a vacuum:

- Does this really have to be done?
- Could someone else do it?
- If it must be done and I must do it, is there a way to do it more efficiently?

Stones and Sand

When you begin each day, you've got a pretty good idea of what your to-do list looks like, even if you haven't committed it to paper. But unless you've got firmly established priorities, you're likely to tackle the easiest things on your list first. After all, it makes perfect sense. You do the things that can be knocked off quickly, thinking that once those items are out of the way, you can focus your time and energy on the more difficult, really important things.

Here's the problem. Before long, the day is gone, and although you've been busy, busy, busy all day and you've crossed quite a few things off your list, you haven't made any real progress. You're no closer to your goal—and to a fulfilling life of significance—than you were yesterday, last week, or last month.

Try this experiment. Get a jar—an empty mayonnaise jar is ideal—and collect some stones and some sand. Fill the jar with sand all the way to the top. Now add the stones.

It doesn't work, right?

Now empty the jar, fill it with stones, then pour in the sand. That's much better. The sand simply fills in the spaces around the stones.

The stones represent the tasks that *should* be your priorities—those activities that, step-by-step, will lead you toward the life you want. The sand represents all those little tasks that are eating up your time and crowding out the more important activities. The grains that have fallen to the bottom of the jar are the real time-wasters.

Now start emptying the jar by removing the stones one at a time. Notice how quickly the level of the sand goes down. Removing just one stone makes a much bigger difference than taking out even a few dozen grains of sand.

When you're deciding how to spend your time, think about that jar. Tackle the larger rocks first. If you never get around to the sand, so what? If a grain of sand eventually grows into a big stone, you can deal with it then. Or if you want, at the end of the day, after you've finished dealing with the rocks, take out a couple of grains of sand so you can have the feeling of accomplishment that comes from crossing things off your list. Just be sure to start with the rocks.

A Frog a Day Keeps Procrastination Away

Just as this isn't a time management book, it also isn't a diet book, but we recommend that you eat a live frog every day. Let us explain.

Procrastination is the bitter enemy of accomplishment, but most of us suffer from it to some extent, especially when we're faced with something that is so unpleasant that we simply can't bear the thought of doing it. No one wants to do things that are unpleasant, but that's simply part of life, and putting those things off can sometimes lead to disaster.

So try this. Imagine that every morning, first thing, before you could do anything else, you had to eat a live frog. No matter what happened after that, the rest of the day would definitely be an improvement, right? The worst would be over. But if you knew you had to eat the frog and you kept putting it off, your day would be ruined, and at some point you'd still have to eat the frog.

If there's a tough task that you don't want to face and you're putting it off, think of it as your frog. Eat it early and move on. The task of eating it won't be any more pleasant, but at least the prospect won't color the rest of your day.

We think it's a good idea to eat a live frog every morning, whether it's preparing a weekly financial report that you always dread or spending the thirty minutes on the treadmill that you never get around to. You'll have a sense of accomplishment that will give you energy for the rest of your day, and you'll have moved closer to reaching your goals.

More Help for Setting Priorities

One problem with setting priorities is that most of us are faced with a myriad of things that must be done each day, so deciding what to do first can be a real headache. Now that you're adding steps toward your newly established goals to the mix, there's an even greater temptation to focus on the easy stuff rather than the tasks that would make a bigger difference in your life.

But don't throw in the towel. It's not as hard as it sounds. One of the simplest methods is to divide the items on your to-do list into three categories:

A. Vital
B. Important
C. Nice

Once you've determined which items are As, Bs and Cs, number the items in each category according to how they rank as your true priorities. This is particularly important with B items, because that will almost always be your largest category. Then work your way through the list in alphabetical and numerical order. It's that simple.

There's one caveat, though. Think carefully about how you categorize your B and C activities. Taking your spouse out to dinner might initially seem to fall into the C category, but if you routinely spend all your time and attention on work and advancing your financial goals, eventually you might not have a spouse to wine and dine. If having a happy family life is among your goals, remember our earlier discussion about the importance of plugging in fun, and be sure that date night makes the B list before it moves its way up to the A category.

The most important thing to remember is to focus on what matters and let the trivial things go. Time management guru Alan Lakein advises his followers to stop several times each day to ask, "What is the best use of my time right now?" It's a good way to ensure that you've got your eye on the ball and to get back on track if you find yourself focusing on the grains of sand rather than the stones in your jar.

Also remember that it's not necessary to slog through a fifty-item to-do list each day. There might be days when all your time is spent on a single task or project. Is that the best use of your time? If the task is one that moves you closer to your most important goals, you bet it is.

There is no better example to illustrate the importance of setting priorities than Andrew Carnegie. It's said that the great industrialist once hired a consultant to help him find ways to run his empire more effectively. The consultant followed Carnegie around for a few days, then handed him his report, which consisted of three sentences:

Make a list of everything you have to do.

Do the most important things first.

Do it every day.

Carnegie scoffed at the simple advice, but the consultant suggested that he follow it for a while, then pay whatever fee Carnegie felt the advice was worth. A few weeks later, the consultant received a check for sixty-four thousand dollars, a small fortune at the time.

Finally, if you've established a goal, but the steps necessary to reach it never seem to make it to the top of your to-do list, maybe it's time to step back and reassess. Perhaps it's not the right goal, at least for now, or maybe you're not as committed to it as you thought you were.

Lauren King got out of bed the moment her alarm went off. She wasn't usually a morning person, but today was different. For the first time in a long time, she was genuinely excited about starting the day.

"You're chipper this morning," said Lauren's husband, Greg, over breakfast.

"Absolutely. It's not every day a person starts writing her first novel."

Lauren had wanted to be a writer for as long as she could remember. She'd taken a couple of creative writing courses in college but had opted for the practicality of an accounting major. So far, her career had been marginally enjoyable, but she never got over the desire to write. She'd written a few short stories and had made notes on several ideas for novels, but she'd never taken the plunge. Between her job and her family, there simply had been no time.

A few weeks earlier, her secure accounting career had suddenly hit the skids when the owner of the small firm for which she worked announced plans to shut down. Much to her surprise, Greg had encouraged her to wait a while before looking for another job.

"We'll be okay on my salary for a while," he'd said. "Why don't you take a few months off and write full-time? You've always talked about writing a book, and there will never be a better time than this. You'd have all day at home while the kids are at school. Take the plunge."

Today was the day: her first day as a novelist. She could hardly wait to get started.

After Greg and the kids left, Lauren headed into the family room. Time to get to work. But first she needed a few things.

Two hours later, Lauren returned from the office supply store and began putting away her purchases. It didn't take long to realize that the desk she would be using was not conducive to productivity. Its surface and drawers had become a repository for all sorts of odds and ends, so she set to work getting it in shape. It would be so much easier to work in an organized space.

By the time the kids got home from school, everything was perfect, but her computer still hadn't been turned on. That's okay, Lauren thought. Now she was ready to dig right in tomorrow morning.

The next morning, Lauren was about to head for her work space when she remembered her promise to make cookies for a school bake sale the next day. Better get that out of the way. She could start planning her outline in her mind while she was baking.

By the end of the week, the house was spotless and every imaginable errand had been run, but Lauren had yet to write a single word. That's okay, she thought. Now that I've gotten all that other stuff done, I can really focus.

Monday morning found Lauren at her computer, where she spent two hours outlining the plot of her novel. A dental appointment interrupted her work, and somehow the rest of the day slipped away. On Tuesday, she wrote eight pages, then realized she needed to do some research on Australia, since that's where the story was set. One website led to another, and by the end of the day she'd made quite a few notes on Australia and had also signed up for Facebook, ordered some Christmas gifts online, and investigated writers' organizations in her area. Quite a productive day, she told herself.

As the weeks went by, Lauren felt guilty about her lack of progress, but she defended herself to Greg when he cautiously asked how things were going. Writing is a creative process, she insisted. She had most of the book written in her head. She just hadn't committed it to paper yet.

One Saturday afternoon, Lauren returned from the grocery to find Greg sitting at the kitchen table, paying the monthly bills. A wave of guilt swept over her as she realized how many weeks had passed since she'd brought home a paycheck and how little progress she'd made on her book.

"You know," she began cautiously, "maybe it's time for me to start looking for a job. We can't exist on one income forever."

"We're fine," Greg replied evenly.

"I know, but . . ." But what? She really didn't know where she was going with this conversation.

"Look, Lauren, we can do whatever you want. It was my idea for you to take this time off to write because I thought it was what you wanted, but if it's not, that's fine. You don't *have* to write a book if you don't want to."

"Of course I want to!"

Greg hesitated for a moment. This could be dangerous territory.

"I know you say that, but it doesn't seem like you really mean it. Since you've been home, you've cleaned out all the closets and the garage, you've painted the kids' bathroom, and you've cooked a lot of new recipes. The only thing you haven't done is write. Working on the book seems to be your last priority rather than your first one."

Lauren looked down at her hands and picked idly at a fingernail. He was right, of course.

"I know. I'm not sure what the problem is. I really want to do this, and I think I've got the skills to do it, but what if I'm wrong? I guess that subconsciously, I think that if I never finish the book, I'll never have to face the fact that maybe I'm *not* a novelist. I'd just be one more person with a dusty old manuscript that no publisher wanted to buy."

"That's true," Greg said. "Of course, right now, you're just one more person who thinks she can write a book but has never really tried. Personally, I'd rather have the dusty old manuscript and the knowledge that I'd given it my best shot."

"You make an excellent point, sir!" Lauren said with a smile. "Give me a couple of days to think about it. If I really don't think I'm up for this, at least right now, I'll start writing a new résumé instead."

"Sounds fair to me."

On Sunday afternoon, Lauren pulled into the parking lot of the restaurant where the monthly meeting of the city's authors' organization was held. She had enthusiastically signed on as a member, looking forward to the opportunity to meet some of her fellow writers, but now she was a bit nervous as she arrived for her first meeting. What if all of these people had written multiple best sellers?

Her fears were groundless. The group seemed to include writers at every level of expertise and experience, and the atmosphere was friendly and welcoming. Lauren found herself chatting with a woman named Grace, who said she had recently completed her third novel and had ideas for a fourth one percolating in her head.

"Wow, that's great," Lauren said. "How long have you been writing full-time?"

"Oh, I don't," Grace said. "I teach English at Franklin High School. I just write in my spare time, when I'm not working or driving my kids to soccer and so forth."

Lauren was amazed. "That's incredible," she said. "How do you find the time? I've been at home full-time for a few months, and I still can't find the time to write."

"Well, it's not that you *can't* find the time. It's probably that you're not *making* the time. If writing was really a priority for you, you'd be doing it."

"That's what my husband says," Lauren replied. "So how are you doing it, with a job and a family?"

"I schedule it," Grace said. "I call it my 'sacred time,' and my family knows to respect it. The thing about writers is that most of us seem to really hate writing, because we're the worst procrastinators in the world. For some reason, we'll do anything to avoid actually sitting down and writing. When I started working on my first book, I planned to write for an hour each night after I got my kids into bed. The problem was that I rarely actually wrote anything because I'd find some excuse not to do it—I had to get tomorrow's dinner into the slow cooker, I was too tired, my favorite movie was on television. There was always an excuse."

"So what did you do?"

"I reordered my priorities. I decided that writing would be the first thing I did every day, before other things started pulling away my attention. Now I get up at five-thirty every morning and write for two hours."

"*Five-thirty?* Yikes, that's early."

"I know, but I'm used to it now. My husband gets the kids up and dressed while I'm squirreled away in our home office, then we all have breakfast together before we head out for the day. I'd like to get a little more sleep, but this has proved to be the only way for me to prioritize my writing. If I don't get it done first thing, I usually don't get it done at all. The other thing I've found is that it gives me momentum for the rest of the day. I find it easier to prioritize the other things I have to do."

"That makes sense," Lauren said. "I guess I'd always assumed that novelists spent eight hours a day at it, kind of like a regular job. I think that's one reason I've found it so hard to get started or get any momentum going. If I don't have that much time to devote to it, it doesn't seem worth getting started if I'm going to have to stop in an hour or two to pick up my kids or whatever."

"You'd be surprised at what you can accomplish in an hour or two," Grace said. "Sometimes I find that I get more done when I have less time because I *have* to work on what's most important and avoid wasting time. When school is out during the summer and I'm at home full-time, I don't write much more than I do during the school year—maybe an extra hour a day, but rarely more than that. As long as I make that two-hour stint in the morning my top priority, it gets done, even if I'm just chipping away little by little."

A month later, Lauren was back at the authors' club, pouring herself a cup of coffee before finding a seat for the meeting, when Grace approached her.

"Hi! How's your book coming?" Grace asked. "Are you making any progress?"

"Amazing progress, actually," Lauren replied. "I gave it a lot of thought after we talked last month, and I decided that I needed to either decide that I wasn't a writer after all or make it a priority and see what happened. I've finished my first draft, and now I'm making some edits and trying to figure out how to start making the rounds to publishers."

"That's great! So are you getting up at five-thirty like I do?"

"Heavens, no! I'm not a morning person, although I guess I'll have to do that if I go back to the corporate world. I start writing at eight-thirty, as soon as my husband and kids are out of the house. I'm not as disciplined as you are, so I have to make some deals with myself. I'm not allowed to have a second cup of coffee until I've worked for thirty minutes, and I can't do the breakfast dishes until I've worked for two hours. That sounds stupid, but I'm a little obsessive about having a clean kitchen, so oddly enough, that's an incentive for me."

"Hey, whatever works!" Grace said. "I work with a guy who gets his wife to hide the sports section from him until he's finished a three-mile run. Hey, would you like me to see if my publisher would be willing to read your manuscript? Can't hurt to ask."

With so many things to distract us from what we need to do, setting priorities and sticking with them isn't easy. There's always e-mail to be checked and rechecked, a great game on TV, your list of bookmarked websites, the little project that will take only a few minutes, and a hundred other things that keep us from getting where we want to go.

But as Lauren is learning, failing to focus on what's most important steals not only our time but also our dreams. Start today to work on your stones before getting sidetracked by all the sand in your jar. You'll be surprised at how attainable even the most ambitious goals will become.

Believe in Belief

What you believe yourself to be, you are.
—*Claude M. Bristol*

As we New York Mets fans used to say during the 1973 baseball season, "Ya gotta believe!" Belief is a feeling of certainty—specifically, being certain of possibilities. When we believe something, what we really believe is that it is *possible*. Whether it's life after death, a cure for cancer or lupus or AIDS, or success in any endeavor, either we believe it's possible or we don't. *Impossibility* might simply be defined as "the absence of positive belief."

The more certain you feel that something is possible for you, the stronger your belief is. Conversely, you can weaken or even kill a belief by introducing doubt.

Doubt is like black paint, and belief is like white paint. Have you ever mixed white paint into black to get gray? It takes an extraordinary amount of white added to black to lighten it, yet the tiniest dab of black added to white makes it gray immediately. Doubt is that strong.

For more than a hundred years, the holy grail of athletic competition was to run a mile in less than four minutes. With each failed attempt, the possibility of success faded further—not simply further into the future, but further from the idea that such a thing was even possible.

From the 1920s to the early 1950s, science and what passed for sports medicine held that the human body was simply incapable of such unbelievable performance. The conventional wisdom of the day was that the lungs could not process enough oxygen to sustain the effort; they would burst under the strain, and so would the heart. Bones would fracture, joints rupture, muscles give out, and ligaments and tendons tear and fail under such stress. It was a physiological and psychological barrier. A human being running a mile in less than four minutes was just *not possible.*

Then on May 6, 1954, in Oxford, England, a young medical student named Roger Bannister ran a mile in 3 minutes and 59.4 seconds.

Obviously, Bannister believed it was possible—and with his historic run, he broke not only the physical four-minute barrier but also a universally held "belief barrier." Within three years, another runner had duplicated Bannister's feat, and in the years that followed, hundreds of others did, too.

What were they all waiting for?

Today, *thousands* of runners around the world have run a mile in less than four minutes. Even high school students do it. Bannister proved it was possible. Now everyone believes it. "Impossible" is something we *make up.*

Clearly, belief is powerful!

Feeling Is Believing

Although our beliefs are feelings of certainty, that doesn't mean that our beliefs are absolute truth. However, we operate *as though* our beliefs are the truth. And isn't it wonderful? It means we can change our beliefs whenever we want. We are in control—in fact, our beliefs are among the few things in life we truly *can* control. In the realm of belief, we are all truly free.

A woman named Janice was in Peter's relationship marketing organization. Janice was a legal secretary and had started her own relationship marketing business because she was fed up with her boss telling her what to do.

Janice had a fantastic opportunity to expand her new enterprise quickly, because she knew at least a hundred successful lawyers who could have served as perfect prospects for her fledgling business. But she didn't contact them.

Peter spent a good amount of time with Janice, and although she had great intentions, week after week, she continued not to get any results. Finally, he asked her, "Janice, what do you think is missing in your approach?" She hemmed and hawed, as though afraid to articulate the real reason for her suboptimal performance. Eventually, however, after enough trust had been established, she confided that she didn't feel on the same level as the professionals for whom she'd once worked as a secretary. She didn't believe that they would treat her as an equal or pay attention to the opportunity she was offering them. Janice was a prisoner of her own beliefs.

Peter had quite a different perspective. He'd *been* a lawyer, and he had gotten out of the profession because he hated it. He also knew what it was like being faced with ethical questions almost every day of his life, and in order to succeed in the legal profession (that is, keep his job), he constantly had to make choices that compromised his integrity. He didn't like that at all.

He shared these thoughts and feelings with Janice on a number of occasions. One day, on the telephone, she suddenly exclaimed, "Peter, I got it! What I'm offering these guys is *hope*. I've got the solution to their problems. These lawyers *need* me!"

At that moment, Janice simply shifted her belief about lawyers and who she really was for them. She shifted her belief from a limiting one to an empowering one. The process of laying the foundation for that moment had taken her two months. In the next six months, she became a transformed person: poised, confident, and self-assured—and her income increased from zero to more than ten thousand dollars a month.

Your Beliefs Are Your Destiny

Your beliefs shape your actions. Your actions cause results—the circumstances of your life—and those results, when stretched out over a lifetime, are what's called your *destiny*. Therefore, your beliefs—what you cause your mind to think and feel certain about—are the causative source of your destiny.

Stop and think for a moment. Is that the way you think it works? For many people, this is a dramatic shift in their way of thinking. Most of us walk around believing that when we earn a hundred thousand dollars, drive a Porsche, or live in a fantastic house, then we'll really feel great!

We think that our results cause our feelings. Although it can work that way, it's not the *only* way. Obviously, things happen and you feel one way or another about them. That's a choice you have. But do you see that your feelings can also cause results?

Remember, your beliefs are *feelings of certainty*—feelings that, however aware or unaware you might be of them, you choose to have. Your feelings direct your actions. So if you want to achieve a specific result, one surefire way to get it is to feel the way you would if that result were already present and true for you.

How would you feel if you earned a hundred thousand dollars? Can you think of any better way to bring that kind of income into your life as fast as possible than feeling like a hundred-thousand-dollar-income earner? There isn't any. It all starts with belief. How would it feel to be able to live beyond your daily stress? How would it feel to be able to give abundantly and generously to your church, family, or even strangers? How would it feel knowing that you could help your parents retire with dignity?

Belief is a powerful tool. This is not "positive thinking" mumbo jumbo; it's how great accomplishments actually occur. It's how success happens, and it's crucial that you understand this point—or at least try it on as a *possibility*.

Knowing this is not enough. Knowledge alone never produces accomplishment. One of the greatest half-truths (that is, half-lies) in the world is "knowledge is power." Not quite.

Do you remember from your high school science days the two types of energy: potential and kinetic? Potential energy is just that, potential. It just sits there, accomplishing nothing. Kinetic energy is energy in action. It's actually doing something.

It's the same with the energy of knowledge. Knowledge in action is kinetic. It's moving and shaking, not just sitting there in your mind. What quality breaks the inertia of potential knowledge's tendency to just sit there, doing nothing, and turns it into wisdom in action? Belief.

The number-one belief for all high achievers and genuinely happy people we have ever met or studied is the belief that *action supersedes everything*.

This is another fundamental shift for many of us: it means changing the habitual strategy of "Ready, aim, fire" to the more proactive—and, most people would assume, more reckless and dangerous—"Fire, aim, ready!" But that's precisely the kind of shift that generates quantum leaps and breakthroughs in our lives.

The Two Types of Beliefs

Beliefs come in two forms: empowering and limiting; these are also referred to as possibility and no-possibility. People commonly think of these as positive beliefs and negative beliefs.

Remember how Janice shifted her beliefs from negative to positive, from limiting to empowering, and the results she achieved when she did? That's the power of adopting possibility beliefs. Of course, Janice had all the inside-track lawyerly information from Peter.

All the runners had the fact that Roger Bannister had already run a 3-minute, 59.4-second mile to bolster their courage. But Bannister didn't. How did he form such a powerful belief while the rest of the world held tenaciously to its limiting one?

The answer is surprisingly simple: he made it up. He made up a challenge and then believed it would happen.

You might say that Peter made up those beliefs for Janice, and you'd be right, because he did. There was just as much evidence that lawyers love their work as there was that they don't. What served Janice was for Peter to make up beliefs that supported her seeing herself as a contribution to those lawyers. Making it up is powerful.

This is one of the great inspiring secrets to success in every aspect of life and work. You make up your beliefs. *You* decide. Positive or negative, you choose to believe what and how you do. It's the possibility we *believe* in that matters, and we discover possibilities even when we have the most limiting evidence at hand. We have a choice: develop beliefs that limit or develop beliefs that inspire. It really is that simple.

So how do you do that? The first thing is, *don't try*!

Trying Is *So* Trying

Since belief is a feeling of certainty based on possibility, and since it seems so very true that humans can do only what they believe they can do, this puts the kibosh on the word *try*.

Look for a pen or a pencil, or any small object, near you. Now *try* to pick it up.

What happened? If this doesn't make sense to you, then don't just read it—really, go ahead, *try*. Don't actually pick it up—that would be *doing*. Don't do it, just *try* to do it. Do you see the difference? *Doing* is in the action. *Trying* is inaction and procrastination. In the words of the *Star Wars* Jedi knight Yoda, "Luke, you either do, or you do not—there is no 'try.'"

We suggest that you get out your dictionary and draw a big line through the word *try*. Then do the same with the word in your own vocabulary. Now let's get back to how to develop beliefs that give you power and how to rid yourself of limiting beliefs.

Asking the Right Questions

One thing that's common to all the high achievers we've met is that they ask themselves questions that help them to develop beliefs that inspire and encourage.

For example, what kind of question is "Why am I so fat?" Is it a limiting question or a powerful question? Look at the possibilities for an answer to that question. They're all limiting: "I'm a pig." "I have no willpower." "I just can't stop eating." "My whole family is fat." No matter what you say, you're trapped. You're either a failure or a helpless victim—probably both.

Ask the question this way instead: "What action could I take to lose twenty pounds and enjoy the process?" Now what happens with your answer? You begin to consider the possibilities. You start looking at possible solutions, exploring new and inspiring ideas. Maybe you even begin to make up some new beliefs for yourself.

It's a whole new and different ball game. It's a high-achieving question that can be answered only by high-achieving possibilities.

One key to establishing new beliefs in yourself—and in others, too—is to ask questions that elicit positive possibility answers. For example, turn "Why can't I quit smoking?" into a positive by asking, "What steps can I take to be smoke-free"? Or turn "What would I do if I lost my job?" into "What alternatives exist to give me the work security I want and deserve?"

In each of these instances, the answers shift from those that serve only to strengthen your negative beliefs and limitations of no possibility into those that strengthen your aspirations and desires and that generate new beliefs for what is possible for you to achieve.

Two little kittens discovered a big pail of cream. Being kittens, they both tried everything they could to get to all that delicious cream. They finally did—and they fell in! At first they were both in kitty heaven, swimming around in the cream, lapping it up, drinking more and more and more. But after drinking their fill, they suddenly realized that they couldn't get out! They tried and tried, but the rim of the pail was just too high to reach.

About this time, their kitten playmates came along and gathered around the rim of the big pail, shouting and jeering at the two kittens in the cream. They made fun of them, mocked them, and laughed at how stupid and foolish they were to fall into the pail of cream, where they couldn't get out.

One kitten kept looking up at the others making fun of him and felt more and more dejected. He kicked and flailed his legs and paws, but to no avail. Finally he gave up and sank exhausted into the cream.

The other kitten also kept looking up at her playmates, but she seemed to be renewed by their taunts and kept trying to jump up and reach the edge of the pail. Eventually all her jumping about turned the cream to butter. She then stood on the firm surface and jumped up and out of the pail easily.

When she got out and stood next to the other kittens, one of them leaned over and asked, "How come you kept trying even though we were laughing at you, making fun of you, and telling you you'd never make it?"

"Oh," replied the kitten in surprise, "you see, I'm a little hard of hearing. I thought you were cheering me on, and that inspired me to keep trying."

We believe very strongly in the power of encouragement. Using the belief principle means becoming "hard of hearing" to any and all limiting beliefs you may encounter. It's simply a numbers game. More bad news leads to limiting beliefs. More good news leads to powerful beliefs. The best news of all is that we can choose what news we get.

You've probably heard about the power of affirmations. They work—and the reason they work so well is that they are simply positive talk that is sent into the subconscious on such a regular basis that they actually reprogram the way you think and feel about yourself. We do not believe in affirmations that are nothing more than lies, because lies don't work. If you're broke and don't want to be broke anymore, don't bother with affirmations like "I'm rich!" That's called delusion; it's a lie. If you're broke, the most powerful affirmation is "I'm broke, and I don't like it! It stops now! I'm done being broke!"

That's all you have to do to discover new, powerful beliefs in yourself. It also works for replacing limiting beliefs with positive, supportive messages.

Although this is a truth people often forget, you have control over what you think. In fact, like the choice of what you believe, the choice of what to think is one of the very few things over which you truly do have control. It determines your beliefs, which dictate what is or is not possible for you to accomplish in your life.

Some personal growth and development teachers and trainers say to "focus on the results." We don't say this because it hasn't worked for us. What has worked for us is to focus on our beliefs and on what's possible, to ask powerful and inspiring questions, and to think thoughts that encourage and inspire.

Your thoughts and feelings inspire the results you accomplish in your life. When your thoughts and feelings are, in some unexplainable way, aligned with what is right and true, they simply proceed toward an inevitable conclusion that you call the result.

Do you want to feel wonderful? Think wonderful. Don't assume that once you've achieved certain hoped-for or anticipated results, the wonderful feeling will follow. That's the big lie. Positive thoughts and feelings are not the *effect* of positive results. They are the *cause*.

Just try—remember that?—to walk around depressed, dejected, and angry at life for throwing dirt in your face, and see what you get: more dirt! It just doesn't work any other way. Want dirt? Ask for it. Want gold instead? Change the question.

When Hunter Anderson arrived home from work, he found his wife, Anna, sitting in stunned silence at their kitchen table. The telephone receiver was in front of her, and she didn't seem to notice as he entered the room.

"Anna? You okay?" he asked.

She looked up, startled, and shook her head.

"No. Nothing is okay. My mother has lung cancer. Lung cancer. I can hardly even say it out loud," Anna replied.

"Lung cancer? How can that be? She's never smoked a cigarette in her life, and neither has anyone in your family."

"I know. It seems impossible, but apparently it happens."

"What's her prognosis?"

Anna sat for a moment, then teared up for the first time since getting the phone call. "It's not good. The doctor said she has maybe four to six months, and that's with aggressive treatment. He's talking about surgery, chemo, radiation—it's just a nightmare," she said.

"There must be something more. That can't just be it," Hunter said.

"Dr. Olson is the best oncologist in the area," Anna replied. "If he thinks there's no hope, there's no hope. Four months! Jenna's birthday is in May. My mother might not be here for Jenna's birthday. She's never missed one of the kids' birthdays, not even when she broke her leg and was in a cast up to her hip, remember? I can't believe this is happening."

The next few days were a blur. Anna's relationship with her mother had always been extremely close, and it seemed impossible that it was coming to an end. She navigated her daily routines as though she were sleepwalking; her stomach was clenched into a knot of fear, dread, and hopelessness. Hunter tried to be supportive, but he felt helpless. He could pick up dinner on his way home from work, help the kids with their homework, and be there when Anna needed someone to talk to, but in the end, it wouldn't matter. His mother-in-law would die soon, and there was nothing he could do to stop it.

Anna accompanied her mother on her next visit to the oncologist, and it did nothing to calm her fears or raise her spirits. The waiting room was filled with patients wearing scarves or hats to cover heads now bald from chemotherapy treatments, and the rack in the corner held brochures about hospice care and how to make a living will. Anna tried to stay upbeat for her mother, but she could barely pay attention as the doctor reeled off a daunting treatment plan beginning with an aggressive surgical procedure scheduled for the next morning. "Have her at the hospital by six," he said. Anna nodded numbly as he described what to expect in the coming days. This couldn't be happening. What was the point? Her mother was going to die anyway.

At nine the next morning, Anna found herself sitting alone in a hospital room, minutes after kissing her mother good-bye as she was wheeled off to surgery. "She might die on the table," she thought. "I might never talk to her again."

As Anna stared vacantly out the window, engrossed in her thoughts, her family's longtime minister tapped softly on the door.

"Hey there," Reverend Bardwell said. "I was hoping to catch your mother before her surgery, but I got caught in traffic. Have they already taken her?"

"Yes, a little while ago." Anna wasn't really in the mood for company.

"How are you holding up?" Reverend Bardwell asked.

"Not well, to be honest," Anna replied. "I've never faced anything remotely like this, and I'm not sure I'm up to the task. I just really don't know where to turn."

Reverend Bardwell smiled slightly. "Well, you can probably predict what I'm about to say. Have you thought about turning to God? If there were ever a time to believe, this is it."

"I know, I'm trying, but I keep thinking about what Mom's doctor said. He hasn't given us much hope at all, and he's the expert. He's seen hundreds of cases like hers, and he says there just aren't many good outcomes."

"Then it's time to turn to a higher power than the doctor," Reverend Bardwell replied quietly.

They talked for more than an hour. The minister recounted stories about situations in which steadfast belief had triumphed over difficult, even seemingly impossible situations. He reminded Anna about stories of faith from the Bible, and he told her about people from their own church who had used their strong beliefs to overcome immense obstacles. It sounded good, but medicine was science. Surely that was stronger than any kind of belief.

Before he left, Reverend Bardwell pulled a small spiral notebook from the pocket of his jacket. He jotted down the author and title of a book on visualization techniques, and underneath he wrote, "If thou canst believe, all things are possible to him that believeth" (Mark 9:23).

Ripping off the sheet of paper and handing it to Anna, he said, "Repeat that a few times when you start to feel hopeless. I think you'll see a difference."

During the next few days, keeping vigil at the hospital, Anna had plenty of time on her hands. To her surprise, she'd found the book Reverend Bardwell had suggested in the hospital gift shop, and she read it from cover to cover, making a few notes in the margins here and there. As her mother slept in her room or dozed off during chemo treatments, Anna visualized thousands of tiny little creatures racing through her mother's body and eagerly gobbling up cancer cells like the figures in the Pac-Man games her son, Zack, played. Sometimes she pictured her mother bathed in a healing white light. She repeated the Bible verse Reverend Bardwell had given her and found other similar passages about the power of belief. They were comforting.

As the days passed, Anna started to feel lighter and stronger, and gradually she began to believe that perhaps the situation wasn't as dire as it seemed. Medical miracles happened all the time, didn't they? As though on cue, the oncologist reported that the combination of surgery, radiation, and chemo had reduced the mass in her mother's lung more than he had expected. It wasn't gone, but it was definitely smaller, maybe small enough to buy her an extra month or two. Anna was elated. Maybe she should learn a little more about her mother's illness. She wasn't a doctor, but a little research might help her know what to expect as the cancer progressed.

While her children were at school each day, Anna began searching the Internet, looking for more information on lung cancer in nonsmokers. One website led to another, and as she learned more, her belief that her mother's condition wasn't hopeless continued to grow and strengthen. The numbers weren't promising, and certainly there were tragic cases, but there were success stories, too. More and more, Anna came to believe that the answer was out there somewhere, and she was determined to find it.

It was a Thursday morning when she landed on the website of a well-known cancer center in New York City. An oncologist there had just gotten approval for a new clinical trial for patients with nonsmoker lung cancer, and he was looking for subjects. Anna glanced quickly through the parameters, then read them again more carefully. Her mother appeared to be a perfect candidate.

By the time she told Hunter about the trial that evening, doubts had begun to creep in. "She can't do this by herself, but

I don't know who could go with her. My sister's baby is due almost anytime, and I can't leave you and the kids," she said.

"Not that long ago, you were telling me that there was no hope for your mother," Hunter responded. "Now there seems to be at least some chance that she can get better. Your belief has gotten you this far. Let's figure it out."

A few weeks later, Anna and her mother were back in the hospital, but this time it was a bright room with a view of Manhattan. Looking back, Anna smiled in amazement. Hunter had been right. Neighbors and church members had stepped forward with amazing speed when they'd learned about the situation. Dinners appeared on the Andersons' table every night, and the refrigerator door sported a carpool schedule to take the children to their games and other after-school activities.

Fifteen-year-old Jenna had grudgingly taken over the family's laundry, and so far she'd ruined only one item. Hunter had figured out how the vacuum worked, and Zack was in charge of loading and unloading the dishwasher. The house didn't run like clockwork as it did when Anna was in charge, but everyone was still alive, and the essentials were getting done.

But the biggest change had taken place in Anna. From the moment she had learned of the clinical trial, she'd hardly recognized herself. She, who normally was short on patience, had stayed on hold for twenty minutes until her call to the oncologist's office had been answered. She, the big-picture person who usually left the details to others, had meticulously filled out the reams of paperwork required before her mother could be considered for the program. She, who famously hated to fly, had eagerly boarded the flight to New York. She, who had always been a bit intimidated by anyone in the medical profession, arrived at the hospital each morning with a list of questions about her mother's treatment, her progress, and what might lie ahead. Through it all, she continued to affirm her belief that her mother could—no, *would*—be helped.

Five months later, Hunter was sitting at the kitchen table, reading the baseball scores, when Anna burst into the house. "It's gone!" she said. "It's really gone! We just came from Mom's PET scan, and it was clean!"

"Really? That's fantastic!" Hunter replied.

"Isn't it? The doctor warned us that cancer is tricky and there are no guarantees, but right now it's actually gone," Anna said, still looking a bit amazed.

"How is that possible?" Hunter asked.

"I don't know," Anna said. "It all seemed so hopeless at first, then it just turned around. The surgery, the radiation, the chemo, the trial—I guess the combination worked somehow."

"I think you can claim a little credit for yourself," Hunter said. "It didn't turn around until you started believing that it could, and you made the rest of us believe it, too. If you had continued to just wallow in hopelessness, you would never have found the clinical trial and pursued it so aggressively. We probably need to tuck that lesson away for the future. I'm sure it will come in handy again someday. Now I'm going to see if Zack wants to go to the batting cage before dinner."

"Not so fast," Anna said. "Jenna's sixteenth birthday is next week, and she's got big expectations. We've got a party to plan."

I'll bet Anna could relate to Walt Disney. Her belief didn't turn an orange grove into a multimillion-dollar entertainment paradise, but once she learned to trust her belief, it was no less powerful than Disney's. She dared to believe in something that had previously seemed impossible, and her belief led to action.

Strengthen Your Commitment

A chicken and a pig were having a discussion. The chicken said, "I am committed to giving one egg every day." "That's not commitment," the pig said. "That's just participation. Giving bacon, now that's commitment!"

Of all the quotes about commitment I've heard or read, the following one, from W. H. Murray's *The Second Himalayan Expedition*, inspires me most:

Until one is committed there is always hesitancy, the chance to draw back, always ineffectiveness. Concerning all acts of initiative, there is one elementary truth, the ignorance of which kills countless ideas and splendid plans: that the moment one definitely commits oneself, then Providence moves too. All sorts of things occur to help one that would never otherwise have occurred. A whole stream of events issues from the decision, raising in one's favor all manner of unforeseen incidents and meetings and material assistance, which no man could have dreamt would have come his way.

I have learned a great respect for one of Goethe's couplets: "Whatever you can do, or dream you can, begin it. Boldness has genius and power in it."

Isn't that wonderful?

Is there anyone who wouldn't love to have "all manner of unforeseen incidents and meetings and material assistance" on his or her side to help along the journey of happiness?

Nothing happens without commitment. Commitment is the secret ingredient in every recipe for success and fulfillment. Once you are committed to something, it happens. No matter how long it takes, no matter what else happens, *no matter what*. That's the power of commitment. It's truly awe-inspiring!

Commitment Is What You Say Will Be Done

Let's have an experience of commitment that really brings home what commitment means. So do this exercise. Ask yourself, "Will my children [and if you don't have kids, use your spouse or your parents] ever starve to death?" Take this question seriously. What's your answer?

We have never met anyone who said anything other than "No! Never! Not a chance!" And everyone says it immediately, apparently without any thought or hesitation at all.

Here's the interesting thing: you have nothing to back up that statement. The truth is, you really don't know what's going to happen tomorrow—or the day after or two hundred days from now. How could you possibly control the future? You can't. There is absolutely no evidence whatsoever that your kids (spouse, or parents) will not starve—yet you will state with total certainty that it will never happen to them. How can you do that?

You do it because you are *committed* to it. That's all. There is no more to it than that.

This is commitment at its clearest and most compelling. It has nothing to do with *how* a thing will or will not be accomplished. Commitment is simply, powerfully, and without question what you say will be done. The how of it all doesn't matter at all to the making of the commitment itself. Commitment has nothing to do with how. Commitment is what will happen no matter what.

To What Are You Committed?

We're going to make a bold assertion: whatever you have in your life right now and whoever you are in your life right now are exactly what you are committed to—no more and no less.

Like belief, attitude, purpose, and all of the other qualities we've been writing about in this book, commitment itself has no color of its own. The color of your commitment is the color you give it. You can be committed to failure or committed to success. It's up to you.

You are always committed to something. The only question is, to what? If you are more committed to your comfort than you are to achieving your goals, you will be comfortable, and you may or may not accomplish your goals. In fact, you might be so committed to your comfort that your goals become impossible, for there are times (most times, really) when we must get out of our comfort zone in order to reach for our aspirations.

Let's think back to our discussion of fear for a moment. Have you ever spoken in front of a sizable group of people? It's considered by most psychologists to be the number-one fear of all time. Why do you suppose that is?

As we noted earlier, most people have a huge, even monstrous, fear of looking bad. Can you imagine anything worse than making a fool of yourself in front of hundreds of people? Would you be willing to be introduced with great fanfare to a big audience and then bomb, let them all down? We wouldn't—and we're certain that you wouldn't, either.

So what's the real problem here? The problem is what the speaker is committed to. In the case of people who are scared to death to speak in front of a group, the problem is that they are committed to looking good, to doing it right, to not blowing it. They are locked in their comfort zone, and that's what they're really committed to: comfort.

What if, instead, you were committed to inspiring and encouraging everyone in the room—would that make a difference? We promise you that it would. It has for us.

Peter's career requires that he speak to large groups of people on a regular basis. At first, that scared his socks off. He was not in his comfort zone at all. The reason he was so frightened was that he was more committed to doing it right and looking good than he was to the men and women who had come to see and hear him or to what they needed and wanted. He was interested in their thinking well of him. He wanted to be "good"—not for them, really, but for himself. He wanted to be liked, appreciated, and recognized, considered important and maybe even famous. It was all about him and his ego. That's what he was committed to.

When he finally got the message to commit to serving the audience, to inspire, encourage, and commit to others' success more than to his own, he became a successful speaker. Before that time, he was too committed to himself to be of much use to others.

Commitment is powerful. Whether it's for you or against you, it is, as always, up to you.

Have you ever met anyone committed to failure? We have— far too many times for our liking. And when you see a person who is committed to success, you sure can tell, can't you?

Have you ever seen an entire company or enterprise committed to success? It's amazing. (Remember the story about Nordstrom?) You can almost feel its commitment, and it's not just superficial optimism and cheering, either. You just know it's going to succeed, and the reason you know that is that it is living and working its commitments.

Do you remember the children's story *The Little Engine That Could?* Kids love it when the little engine begins chugging up the long steep hill, pulling the circus train behind it, affirming again and again, "I think I can, I think I can." That little engine is *committed.*

Most people are committed to convenience and comfort. Are you? Winners, in contrast, are committed to success, high achievement, happiness, and fulfillment. Are you?

The next question is, "How do I get committed?"

The Meaning of Commitment

First, let's have a clear understanding of what commitment really means.

Commitment is not necessarily a do-or-die affair; you don't have to throw yourself onto railroad tracks in service of your goal to prove you're committed to it. And you don't need to commit hara-kiri if you fail to reach a declared goal when or how you said you would.

When you are committed to something, you simply agree to play fully—win, lose, or draw. If you have committed to spending the evening playing a board game with your spouse and children, you don't blow it off because you suddenly realize that your favorite movie is on TV. You play the game, and you do it with a good spirit, because you said you would do it. If you have committed to making ten sales calls to new people this week, and it's Friday afternoon and you've made only nine, you don't trot off to play eighteen holes of golf. You make the tenth call, because you said you would. Commitment is as simple as giving and keeping your word and doing your best. Commitment is doing what you said you would do, whether you feel like it or not.

Do you remember the baseball player Reggie Jackson? Reggie's nickname was "Mr. October" because that's when the World Series is played—and no matter what, Reggie would come through in those championship games. Once he hit two home runs in a World Series game with a 104-degree temperature and a bad case of the flu. That's why Reggie is in the Baseball Hall of Fame—Mr. October, Mr. Commitment.

Do you remember when President John F. Kennedy committed the entire country to landing a man on the moon in only ten years? "I believe," Kennedy said, "this nation should commit itself to achieving the goal of putting a man on the moon before this decade is out."

Crazy, right? At the time it sure was. The United States was way behind the Russians in the space race, but the *Eagle* landed with a giant step for mankind—and right on schedule, too. America, the land of the free—and committed.

Scratch any happy, fulfilled person from any walk of life, and just beneath the surface you will find the thread of commitment that is common to all of them. People are simply attracted to those who can be counted on to honor their commitments, no matter what.

Leaders Leverage Power

In the business world, the fast lane on the highway of success is the lane of leadership, because accomplishment through others is a major key to success. This secret to leadership is summed up in a statement attributed to Andrew Carnegie: "I would rather have 1 percent of the efforts of a hundred people than 100 percent of my own."

That's because leverage works. You can achieve a hundred times more through a team or network of people than you can ever do all by yourself. No man or woman is an island, and the nature of people is that they will do what you do and do what you say, if you are a person who keeps his or her word—in other words, if you are committed.

Leadership is the fast lane. People will follow you if you are committed.

You must make a commitment before you ask for one. Commit to your dream the way a baby commits to walking. The child tries and tries and tries again until he or she walks. There is no maybe, no stopping, no comfort zone, there is only doing—walking.

Remember, we do not get paid for what we know, we get paid for *what we do* with what we know. We don't get paid for *who* we know, either. We get paid for *what we can accomplish* with and through whom we know. And the doing of both of these, and anything else that matters, requires commitment.

Ed McElroy of U.S. Air once said, "Commitment gives us new power. No matter what comes to us—sickness, poverty, or disaster—we never turn our eye from the goal."

Stew Leonard is the owner of "the world's largest dairy store" in Norwalk, Connecticut. His store began as a thousand-square-foot, mom-and-pop retail operation, and it has grown to more than a hundred thousand square feet with annual sales of at least a hundred million dollars from just one store. Now Leonard has branched out to open other stores in Connecticut and New York.

Early in his business, Stew placed a three-ton rock beside the front door of his store. Chiseled in the rock is the following statement:

Rule #1: The customer is always right.

Rule #2: If the customer is ever wrong—reread Rule #1.

That's Leonard's commitment—carved in stone for all his customers to read. The motto is chiseled in rock, Leonard says, "because it will never change."

Woody Allen once said that "80 percent of success in life is just showing up." True, perhaps—but "showing up" isn't all there is to commitment. It's the other 20 percent that rules, that has the real power and makes the difference between failure and success. That 20 percent is commitment.

Commitment isn't necessarily a life-or-death matter. If you make a commitment and play fully but don't reach your goal, you're not going to have to give up your firstborn child. When you are committed, you just play the game as *though* your child or something else that really matters to you were on the line.

The great football coach Vince Lombardi once said, "There is only one way to succeed in anything . . . and that is to give everything. I do, and I demand that my players do. Any man's finest hour is when he has worked his heart out in a good cause and lies exhausted on the field of battle . . . victorious."

It's about commitment.

Finally, Walter Cronkite said, "I can't imagine a person becoming a success who doesn't give this game of life everything he's got."

Please understand that commitment is not just for leaders. Even though this section of this chapter focused on leadership, commitment is a principle for all of us. We must commit to being good parents, spouses, role models, employers, employees, teachers, students, or anything else we pursue.

Take a moment now to review your values and purpose, and also take another look at your beliefs. Then make a list of the top five commitments you are willing to make right now. Ask yourself the following:

What are you committed to doing?
What kind of person are you committed to being?
What five things would you tell the world you are committed to right now?

Don't give a thought to how you will accomplish these commitments. There'll be time enough for that later on. Write your five commitments below:

1. _____
2. _____
3. _____
4. _____
5. _____

One of the biggest payoffs of being committed to something is persistence. Many people would say that persistence is a tool, a means to an end, but we say it's a reward. Marriage is a great example of how persistence is a reward. The kind of commitment that lasts forever is not easy, but it is its own reward.

One of the most cherished qualities of any associate or friend with whom we've developed a relationship over the years is persistence. Without it, a person is sunk. The skill to stick to it and with it brings more joy and success than almost any other ability we know of.

Persistence truly is its own reward. People often ask, "Well, okay—but how long must I persist?" Just think about that question for a moment. Do you see that it is an oxymoron—a concept that contradicts itself? It's like saying, "I like to be consistent—sometimes."

You simply must persist until you succeed and reach your dreams. Everybody's dreams are different, and no one knows how long the gestation period is for any dream. What we do know, however, is that if you keep focused and committed, you *must* succeed. There is no way to fail unless you give up. Since the only way to fail is to give up, if you persist and do not give up, you will succeed.

The biggest problem most people have with success is that they quit before they achieve it. Did you know that 80 percent of all small businesses fail in their first year, that 80 percent of the rest don't make it to year five, and that 80 percent of the remainders will never see year ten? The biggest problem facing most entrepreneurs is that they quit before payday.

Think about that one, too, for a moment. If you've ever experienced a failure in your life, take another look at it and ask yourself, "Did I quit too soon? What's the possibility that if I had persisted, I would have succeeded?" The chances are excellent that you would have.

Again, persistence is its own reward. It comes from commitment and in turn strengthens it. Persistence is the opposite of giving up, and giving up is really nothing more than a bad habit—a habitude.

It's important to replace the bad habit of giving up with the good habit of persistence. The only way to get rid of a bad habit is by replacing it with a new and better habit, and all it takes to enforce a new habit is twenty-one days of repetition.

Isn't it interesting that the only way to build the habit of persistence is through persistence? A lack of persistence and a lack of commitment can only result in feelings of indifference, indecision, and procrastination.

Here's a favorite quote of ours from Calvin Coolidge that speaks powerfully about persistence:

> Nothing in the world can take the place of persistence. Talent will not; nothing is more common than unsuccessful men with great talent. Genius will not; unrewarded genius is almost a proverb. Education will not; the world is full of educated derelicts. Persistence and determination alone are omnipotent.

Commitment in action is determined and persistent. Commitment is relentless patience. Commitment is what makes the difference. Commitment requires focus, positive belief, a positive attitude, and purpose, and all of these in turn require commitment.

Todd Hurley sat at the dinner table with his brother's family. As he helped himself to more potatoes, he turned to his sister-in-law.

"Jen, I thought I saw you at the courthouse today," he said. "You're not in legal trouble, are you? I might be Bill's little brother, but I'm also a really great lawyer."

"No, I'm fine," Jennifer replied with a laugh. "My women's group at church runs the children's waiting room up in family court, and I've just started volunteering there."

"What's the children's waiting room?" nine-year-old Molly asked.

"It's a place for kids to wait when they have to come to court," Jennifer said. "It gives them a place to hang out and play."

"What did they do to get in trouble and have to go to court?" asked Grant, who was eleven.

"These kids aren't in trouble," Todd said. "They're in court for different reasons. Sometimes they've been hurt by their parents or someone else and the kids have to tell the judge what happened. Some of them don't have a family anymore and the court has to find a place for them to live. The judges are really busy, so sometimes they have to wait a long time, and it's pretty boring. Sometimes the judge wants them to leave the courtroom while he talks to other people about their case, and the waiting room gives them a safe place to go."

"It's nice," Jennifer added. "There are toys and books and people like me to read or play with them. Coming to court can be scary for them, so we try to take their minds off that."

After the children had left the table, Bill, Jennifer, and Todd lingered over coffee. Jennifer brought up the waiting room again.

"My heart goes out to those kids," she said. "Some of them seem so sad, and you really wonder what they've been through in their short lives."

"I know what you mean," Todd said. "I've spent some time in family court. It's amazing how some parents would go to the ends of the earth to take care of their kids but others neglect or even abuse them."

"There was a little girl who spent nearly two hours with us today," Jennifer said. "Her name was Emily and she was adorable, but she had such sad eyes. She was playing a board game with me when her social worker came in and introduced her to her new foster parents. I felt so sorry for her, going off to live with strangers. I can't imagine what that would be like. She didn't seem to be much younger than Grant."

A few days later, Jennifer saw Emily's social worker in the courthouse hallway. She introduced herself and said, "I was wondering how Emily is doing."

"Who?"

"The little girl you were with the other day. Long dark hair, big brown eyes, about eight years old. You were setting her up with a new foster family."

"Oh, right, I think I remember her. My caseload is pretty big. I'm sure she's fine, though. Nice meeting you."

Two weeks later, Jennifer had just unlocked the door to the waiting room when Emily entered, flanked by her foster mother and a woman Jennifer didn't recognize. The woman introduced herself as Emily's social worker. "We're here to have the judge review Emily's placement, so we'll just leave her with you until he's ready for her," she said.

After they left, Jennifer said to Emily, "I thought Ms. Henry was your social worker. The one who was with you the last time you were here."

"I've had a lot of social workers," Emily said simply. "A lot of lawyers, too. I can't even remember their names most of the time."

Jennifer didn't see Emily again for nearly two months, but she thought about her occasionally and wondered how things were working out for her. She mentioned the little girl to one of her fellow volunteers during a slow day in the children's waiting room.

"Oh, I know Emily," the woman replied. "She was in here a few days ago. She was in court to get placed with a new foster family."

"A new family? What happened to the old one?"

"I don't know," she said as she moved to the other side of the room to rearrange a toy shelf.

Jennifer mentioned the conversation to Todd the next time he was at their house for dinner. "Why would she be moved to a new foster home so quickly? She barely had time to adjust to the last one."

"It happens," Todd said with a shrug. "Sometimes the family moves. Sometimes the parents realize that having a foster child just isn't for them. Sometimes there are conflicts if there are other children in the home. It's a shame, but it happens more than you'd like to think."

"That's awful," Jennifer said. "I've been working in the waiting room less than three months, and in that time, that little girl has had at least two social workers and two foster families that I know of, and who knows how many lawyers have handled her case? How is she supposed to have any stability?"

"You seem pretty passionate about this," Todd said.

"I am. It seems so unfair for her to get shuffled around like that."

"Are you interested enough to help her? Or another child like her?"

"Sure, I'd like to, but I don't know what I could do."

Todd told her about a program called Speak Up for a Child that he'd recently learned about at a seminar. The program matched volunteers with children like Emily who were involved in the court system. The volunteer followed the child's case through to the end (when he or she turned eighteen and left the foster or group home system), serving as an advocate to look out for the child's best interests through-out the process. The volunteer attended the child's court hear-ings, provided another set of eyes and ears to ensure that foster placements were working, and tried to become a stabilizing presence in the child's life.

"Do you think you'd have time to do something like that?" Todd asked. "It's not as time-consuming as it sounds. If you're interested, I could get you set up."

Within a few weeks, Jennifer had been accepted as a volunteer, and her request to be assigned to Emily's case had been approved. Her heart broke as she read through the file she'd been given.

Emily's parents had divorced when she was only three years old, and she had never seen her father again. She'd been removed from her mother's home when she was five because her stepfather was physically abusive to her. She couldn't be returned because the stepfather was still living in the home, so she had been bounced around the foster care system for the past three years. Her mother had visitation rights but often did not show up for scheduled visits. No wonder Emily smiled so rarely.

Jennifer's first visit to Emily's current foster home was awkward. The foster mother seemed defensive, resenting the fact that yet another person had been sent to judge her fitness as a parent despite Jennifer's explanation of her role in the little girl's life. Emily was polite but, like her foster mother, seemed a little mistrustful. Telling Bill about the visit later that night, Jennifer said, "To tell you the truth, it hurt my feelings a little bit. I'm just trying to help."

"Well, given everything you said Emily has been through, I'm not surprised she didn't jump into your arms," Bill replied. "She's got plenty of reasons to doubt people's good intentions. You probably just need to hang in there and give her some time."

During the next few months, Jennifer committed herself to chipping away at the little girl's reserve. She invited her over for dinner several times, but Emily always seemed uncomfortable and barely spoke to the other family members. Jennifer attended all of her court hearings and issued thorough reports on her observations of Emily and her foster home. She picked Emily up at school every Wednesday, took her to the library or a nearby park, and helped with her homework before returning her to her foster home. She thought she was making progress, but it was slow.

Nearly eight months after meeting Emily for the first time, Jennifer arrived home to find a message from the little girl's social worker on her answering machine. "I'm sorry this is last-minute, but we've got a court hearing for Emily tomorrow morning. Something has come up, and Judge Walker agreed to put us on her docket. Try to be there at ten, but if you're busy I can explain it to the judge since you didn't have much notice. Thanks. Bye."

Jennifer had trouble finding a parking spot the next morning, so she rushed into the courtroom just as the judge was calling Emily's case. "I guess I'll find out what's going on soon enough," she thought as she took a seat.

A young attorney stood up to speak. "Your Honor, we're here today to make a change in Emily's placement. Her current foster family is no longer able to keep her, so we need to find a new placement for her."

Jennifer looked up in alarm. Emily dropped her head slightly and looked down at the table in front of her.

"What's your recommendation?" Judge Walker asked without looking up.

"We recommend that she be placed in a group home, at least temporarily, until we can reevaluate her case."

"You can't do that!" Jennifer was amazed to find that those words had come out of her mouth.

"I'm sorry, who are you?" the judge asked.

"Jennifer Hurley. I'm Emily's volunteer advocate. I've been working with her for months, and you can't just ship her off to a group home. That's just not right." Jennifer knew she should apologize for her outburst and sit down, but she couldn't do it. She had to stand up for Emily, who had turned around and was staring at her with wide eyes.

"Ms. Hurley, I'm sorry, but you don't have a say in this," Judge Walker said. "I understand that you care about Emily and you're concerned about her, but I can assure you, this court has her best interests at heart also. Her current foster father is being transferred to Chicago, and as I'm sure you know, Emily cannot be moved out of state. Her mother still retains her parental rights, so . . . "

"I understand that," Jennifer interrupted. What are you doing, she asked herself. You're going to be sent to jail for contempt of court. "Look, when I joined this program, I made a commitment to Emily. I promised to be her advocate, and I'm not backing away from that. I've been the only constant in her life for almost a year. She's just started to trust me, and I can't let this happen to her. She doesn't deserve to be shuffled around again, and to a group home? She's only eight years old. That's the best you've got?"

"Ms. Hurley, I admire your passion. I really do, but surely you understand by now that we have more children than the system can handle. Until another foster family becomes available, a group home is the best we can do, unless you've got another suggestion."

"Approve my home as an emergency placement. My husband and I will be happy to take her."

Ten years later, Bill and Jennifer watched proudly as Emily received her high school diploma.

"She turns eighteen in a couple of weeks," Jennifer said. "Then she'll officially graduate from the foster care system, too."

"I wish we could have adopted her," Bill said wistfully. "But she'll always be our daughter even if she isn't legally ours. And just think, when she leaves for college in the fall, we'll be empty nesters."

Jennifer looked at him hesitantly. She'd been wondering how to broach this.

"About that—we've done pretty well with our first three children. How would you feel about a fourth?"

"I think we're a little old to have another baby, Jen."

"I'm not talking about a baby. There's a little boy who's been coming into the children's waiting room that you'd just love."

The Hurleys hadn't planned to expand their family, and when Jennifer volunteered to spend a few hours a week in the children's waiting room, she didn't think it would lead to becoming a mother again. But her commitment to Emily, and to bringing some level of permanence into her fractured life, had steadily grown over several months and had enabled her to step up when Emily needed her most.

So what are you committed to? And what are you willing to do to make it happen? You'll need one final principle in order to follow your commitment all the way to the end. Let's talk about it now.

Make a Choice

The greatest power a person possesses
is the power to choose.
—*J. Martin Kohe*

This principle is a fairly simple one, yet it is extremely powerful, for you must exercise it to gain access to all the others. It is simply the knowledge—not only in theory or in periods of reflection, but moment by moment throughout your day—that it is up to you. It's your *choice*.

It is through choice, not chance, that we forge our futures. We are all in possession of the power to shape our destinies, moment by moment, with choice.

We want to share a story with you that we first heard from peak performance expert Dr. Charles Garfield about a young man named Henry Peterson.

Henry had a dream of being the very first person in his family ever to graduate from college. He applied and was accepted to Georgetown University.

Henry had another dream. He wanted to play college football. He never considered going pro; he just wanted to play for his college team. He tried out for the team and made it.

For four years, Henry sat on the bench. One week before the final game of the season in his senior year, tragedy struck Henry's family. His father died. Henry was torn. If he went home, he let the team down; if he stayed and played, he failed his family.

He asked his coach for advice. The coach told him, "Go home, Henry. Your family needs you more than the team does." So Henry went home.

About an hour before the big game, who showed up in the locker room but Henry, suited up and ready to play! The coach, seeing him there, blew his top. "Henry," he shouted, "I thought I told you to go home!"

"Coach," Henry replied quietly, "I need a favor."

"What?" replied the upset coach. After a moment, he cooled off and told Henry, "Anything, Henry. What do you want?"

"Coach, I need to start the game today."

"What!" said the coach, with some anger returning. "Well, not *anything*, Henry. Look, you've sat on the bench for four years. I can't start you—"

"Coach," Henry repeated firmly, "just this once—please?"

"All right," the coach relented, "but the first time you compromise the team effort I'll take you out, Henry. It's nothing personal. The game is just bigger than you or me."

So Henry started—and he was awesome. He blocked. He faked. He carried the ball play after play after play, gained more than a hundred yards rushing, and scored two touchdowns on the way to helping his team win a resounding victory.

At the end of the game, the coach ran up, gave Henry a bear hug, and screamed, "Henry, Henry, why didn't you tell me you could play like that?"

"Did you ever meet my dad?" Henry asked in return.

"No, son," the coach said, "I never had the pleasure."

"Did you ever see my dad and me walking around the field for hours and hours, talking, arm in arm?"

"No, son," the coach said, and asked, "What's your point, Henry?"

"Coach," said Henry, looking at the older man with tears in his eyes, "my dad was blind. Today was the first game he was ever able to see me play."

Henry fulfilled his dream of being the first in his family to graduate from college, and he went on to build a very successful business career, as well. Henry points to that day and that football game as his shining moment, as the day his life changed for the better—forever. When asked why, Henry says, "Because that was the day I realized it was my choice to be a benchwarmer or a player."

Choice, not chance. That's the key to living a significant life.

Please understand that this is not a choice you make once and you're done. The choice to live a significant life is a moment-by-moment opportunity. You will be presented with the choice again and again and again, thousands and even millions of times throughout your life. Each time it will be new and fresh. Each time you make a choice in favor of a significant life, you will be energized, uplifted, and electrified

Choice is our greatest power. No one can ever take it from us. It is the ultimate gift and the ultimate freedom.

Vernon Howard, the wonderfully pragmatic master of human potential, once said: "You need only choose ... then keep choosing as many times as necessary. That is all you need do. And it is certainly something you can do. Then, as you continue to choose, everything is yours."

Given the choice, we know you will choose to live a significant life.

Just like the rest of us, the characters we've met in our little parables had choices to make.

Justin could have given in to his natural shyness and missed his opportunity to attend space camp, but he chose to let his desire overcome his discomfort and take the necessary steps to achieve his dream.

Brad chose to follow his heart to discover his real purpose, to face down the fear of failure that was keeping him stuck in one place, to sharpen his focus, and to take the first steps toward a life of true significance.

Maria dared to dream of having more personal satisfaction while making a bigger impact on her patients, and she exercised her imagination to make it happen.

David chose to stop drifting and establish the goals that would shape his personal and professional future.

Megan chose to change her attitude, and in the process she brought about improvements in her own life and that of her family.

Chris chose to put aside his leisurely retirement in favor of establishing a new career that would make an enormous difference in the lives of people who desperately needed his help.

Lauren took control of her life by choosing to make her book a priority rather than an unfulfilled dream.

Anna had a choice between giving up, by accepting what seemed to be her mother's fate, and believing that there was still hope. She chose hope.

Jennifer chose to walk the talk. Her choice to follow through on her commitment dramatically changed the life of a child.

So what about you? Every choice you make has a result of some sort, and the choice not to choose is, of course, also a choice. Choose carefully, and you will quickly find yourself on the road to significance.

Epilogue

O n a dark and stormy night, a battleship is returning home to port after maneuvers in the North Atlantic. The seas are stormy and gale force winds are blowing, so the captain of the ship has remained on deck to see the vessel safely to its port.

A battleship is a massive assemblage of hundreds of tons of metal, engines, guns, computers, technology, and people—more than a thousand men and women, in this case. It's like a skyscraper on its side in the water. And tonight this particular skyscraper is tossing up and down in very rough seas.

All of a sudden, the signalman leans onto the bridge and says, "Captain, signal off the port bow."

The captain has only one concern at this point. He asks, "Is it steady or moving astern?"

If the signal is moving astern (toward the back of the boat), all is well; they are simply two ships passing in the night. But if the signal remains steady, that means they're on a collision course.

"Steady, Captain" comes the reply.

"Signal this," barks the captain. "We are on a collision course; suggest you change course twenty degrees.'"

The signalman does so, and the response comes back, "Suggest *you* change course twenty degrees."

It is quite rare for a naval captain to be addressed in such a fashion. But the captain retains his composure and, though a bit aggravated, commands his signalman to send the following: "I am a captain—change course twenty degrees!"

Again, the reply comes back, "I am a signalman second-class—*you* change course twenty degrees."

Now the captain is furious, and he roars the message, "I am a battleship—change course twenty degrees!"

And the signal returns, "I am a lighthouse."

As you're coming to the conclusion of this book, it is our hope that you are feeling like a lighthouse: strong and steady, shining out a bright beacon of light that can be seen for many miles.

We opened this book with a discussion of Social Entrepreneurship, and we now close with a commercial for the same. The world is forever changed. The great global, social challenges will not be solved through traditional giving. It's going to take a new type of thinking. It's going to take a new type of entrepreneur. It's going to take *you*. Social Entrepreneurship may be the answer, and it is the most exciting business model we have seen in our lives. Simply put, it allows ordinary people to make an extraordinary impact. Using for-profit know-how and entrepreneurial drive and wisdom to solve the greatest challenges of our times—that's what it's all about.

Imagine a business model where each time a product is purchased, one is given to a child in need. Imagine a company that is so committed to global change that each time consumers purchase their goods, families are fed. Imagine an industry that is so committed to radical giving that each customer translates into power to the powerless. Now imagine *you* being part of that business, company, or industry. Compassionate Consumption will be a wave of the future. We envision a day where companies around the globe will put a "Compassionate Consumption" seal on their products, and consumers worldwide will support those companies that are making a difference. We welcome you to the world of Social Entrepreneurship and hope you're full of enthusiasm and excitement as you prepare to begin translating the principles we've discussed into a life of true significance.

Together, we will inspire a movement of social entrepreneurs, and empower families around the world to live life to the fullest, retire with dignity, and leave a legacy to future generations. Together, we will give radically, live passionately, and create lives of impact, influence, success, and significance. Together, we will live the significant life.

Index